Total alles über den Schwarzwald

The Complete Black Forest

Herausgegeben mit freundlicher Unterstützung von
Printed with generous support from:

Schwarzwald Tourismus GmbH,
www.schwarzwald-tourismus.info

Dank / Acknowledgements:

Ein besonderer Dank für die großartige Unterstützung bei der Recherche und die redaktionelle Mitarbeit geht an das Presseteam der Schwarzwald Tourismus GmbH: Gaby Baur, Michael Gilg und Wolfgang Weiler. Weiter danken wir herzlich: Toni Schäfer und Alexander Thoma.

Special thanks to Gaby Baur, Michael Gilg and Wolfgang Weiler from the press team at Schwarzwald Tourismus GmbH for their invaluable research assistance and editorial collaboration.
Our sincere thanks as well to Toni Schäfer and Alexander Thoma.

Auch bei Folio erschienen / Also available from Folio:

Hermann Gummerer / Franziska Hack / no.parking:
Total alles über Südtirol / Alto Adige - Tutto di tutto / The Complete South Tyrol

Sonja Franzke / no.parking:
Total alles über Österreich / The Complete Austria

Martin Wittmann / no.parking:
Total alles über Bayern / The Complete Bavaria

Sonja Franzke / no.parking:
Total alles über Wien / The Complete Vienna (pocket edition)

Susann Sitzler / no.parking:
Total alles über die Schweiz / The Complete Switzerland

1. Auflage / 1st edition 2020
© Folio Verlag Wien/Vienna – Bozen/Bolzano
Idee & Konzept / Idea & Concept:
Hermann Gummerer, no.parking
Translation into English: Jennifer Taylor
Lektorat / Proofreading: Hermann Gummerer,
Joe Rabl, Daniel Ostermann
Grafik und Umbruch / Graphic design: no.parking, Vicenza
Prepress: Typoplus, Frangart
Printed in Europe
ISBN 978-3-85256-820-1

www.folioverlag.com

Jens Schäfer ✱ Infographics: no.parking

In Zusammenarbeit mit / In collaboration with: Hermann Gummerer

TOTAL ALLES ÜBER DEN SCHWARZWALD

THE COMPLETE BLACK FOREST

Folio

Inhalt
Index

ABC

Der Autor / Jens Schäfer
Der gebürtige Schwarzwälder lebt in Berlin, wo er Drehbücher, Romane und Sachbücher schreibt. Er ist Autor der „Gebrauchsanweisung für den Schwarzwald" und der Kolumne „Schäfers Schwarzwald", die bis 2018 im Freiburger „Regio Magazin" erschien. Plagt ihn Heimweh, trifft er sich mit Landsleuten auf ein Tannenzäpfle in den Schwarzwaldstuben in Berlin-Mitte.
www.jensschaeferberlin.de

The author / Jens Schäfer was born in the Black Forest and lives today in Berlin, where he writes screenplays, novels and non-fiction. He is the author of the "Instruction Manual for the Black Forest" and wrote the column "Schäfer's Black Forest" for Freiburg's "Regio magazine" from 2015 to 2018. When he gets homesick, he meets his fellow Black Foresters for a Tannenzäpfle beer at the Schwarzwaldstuben in Berlin-Mitte.
www.jensschaeferberlin.de

Die Gestalterinnen / no.parking ist eine Agentur für Kommunikation und Gestaltung in Vicenza: Vier Frauen switchen zwischen deutschem und italienischem Kulturraum hin und her und begreifen Design als etwas, das unser Leben schöner macht, nützlich ist und allen zugänglich sein sollte.
www.noparking.it

The graphic designers / no.parking is an agency for communication and design based in Vicenza. The four women who make up the team switch back and forth between the German and Italian cultural realms and view design as something that makes our lives more beautiful, something that is useful and should be accessible to all.
www.noparking.it

Der Co-Autor / Hermann Gummerer
studierte Germanistik und Philosophie und ist Mitbegründer und Co-Verleger des Folio Verlags.

The co-author / Hermann Gummerer
studied German linguistics & literature and philosophy and is co-founder and co-owner of the Folio publishing company.

Alemannisch: 8, 18, 108
Aussichtstürme: 78
Barbarastollen: 104
Bäume: 26, 28, 30
Benz, Carl Friedrich: 96
Berge: 12
Bibbeleskäs: 18, 52, 54
Bier: 46
Bollenhut: 10, 34
Brägele: 19, 52, 54
Cego: 56
Champagnerflasche: 96
Das kalte Herz: 106, 108
Eisenbahn: 70
Erfinder: 96
Europa-Park: 80
Faller: 36, 70
Farben: 10
Fasnet (Fasnacht): 82
Faust, Dr. Johann Georg: 94
Feldberg: 8, 12, 42, 66, 68, 78, 84
Ferienstraßen: 72
Film: 106
Flüsse: 14
Fußball: 62, 64
Gäste: 84, 86
Geschichte: 58
Grohe: 97
Hinterwälder Rind: 11, 38, 40
Junghans: 97
Kaiserstuhl: 8, 13, 23, 48, 68
Kirchen: 90
Kirschwasser: 50
Klöster: 90
Küche: 52
Kuckucksuhr: 11, 31, 32, 71, 73
Kunst: 100
Literatur: 108
Longinuskreuz: 92
Löw, Jogi: 62, 65
Museen: 100
Nachnamen: 20
Naturparks: 24
Ortsnamen: 16, 28
Prominente: 60, 86
Restaurants: 52
Rottweiler: 41
Sauschwänzlebahn: 70
Schnaps: 50
Schwarzwälder Kirschtorte: 10, 44
Schwarzwälder Schinken: 10, 12, 42
Schwarzwaldhaus: 36
Schwarzwaldverein: 10, 74
Schweizer Wald: 29
Seen: 14

Ski: 66
Spezialitäten: 42, 44, 48, 50, 52, 54
Sport: 66
Sport-Club Freiburg: 10, 62, 64
St. Märgener Fuchs: 11, 40
Staufen: 94
Sterneküche: 52, 81
Straußenwirtschaft: 54
Streich, Christian: 64
Superlative: 22
Tannenzäpfle: 10
Thermalbäder: 88
Tiere: 40
Tourismus: 84
Tracht: 34
Uhrenstraße, Deutsche: 73
Uhu: 10, 96
Vogtsbauernhof: 11, 34, 36
Wald: 26, 28
Wanderwege: 74, 76
Wankelmotor: 97
Wasser: 14
Wasserfälle: 14
Wein: 48
Weltmarktführer: 98
Wetter: 68
Winterhalter, F. X. & H. F.: 102

Alemannic: 8, 18, 108
Animals: 40
Art: 100
Barbarastollen underground archive: 104
Beer: 46
Benz, Carl Friedrich: 96
Bibbeleskäs (curd cheese): 18, 52, 54
Black Forest Cake: 10, 44
Black Forest Ham: 10, 12, 42
Black Forest Hiking Club: 10, 74
Black Forest Horse: 11, 40
Black Forest houses: 36
Bollenhut traditional hat: 10, 34
Brägele fried potatoes: 19, 52, 54
Carnival: 82
Cego card game: 56
Celebrities: 60, 86
Champagne bottle: 96
Churches: 90
Clock Road, German: 73
Colours: 10
Cuckoo clock: 11, 31, 32, 71, 73
Cuisine: 52
Europa-Park: 80
Faller: 36, 70
Faust, Dr. Johann Georg: 94
Feldberg: 8, 12, 42, 66, 68, 78, 84

Film: 106
Folk costumes: 34
Football: 62, 64
Forest: 26, 28
Gastronomic specialities: 42, 44, 48, 50, 52, 54
Grohe: 97
Guests: 84, 86
Heart of Stone: 106, 108
Hiking trails: 74, 76
Hinterwälder Cattle: 11, 38, 40
History: 58
Holiday routes: 72
Inventors: 96
Junghans: 97
Kaiserstuhl: 8, 13, 23, 48, 68
Kirsch: 50
Lakes: 14
Literature: 108
Longinus cross: 92
Löw, Jogi: 62, 65
Monasteries: 90
Mountains: 12
Museums: 100
Nature parks: 24
Observation towers: 78
Place names: 16, 28
Railway: 70
Restaurants: 52, 81
Rivers: 14
Rottweiler: 41
Sauschwänzlebahn (pigtail line): 70
Schnapps: 50
Skiing: 66
Sport: 66
Sport-Club Freiburg: 10, 62, 64
Staufen: 94
Streich, Christian: 64
Superlatives: 22
Surnames: 20
Swiss Forest: 29
Tannenzäpfle beer: 10
Thermal baths: 88
Tourism: 84
Trees: 26, 28, 30
Uhu glue: 10, 96
Vogtsbauernhof open-air museum: 11, 34, 36
Wankel engine: 97
Water: 14
Waterfalls: 14
Weather: 68
Wine: 48
Winery inns: 54
Winterhalter, F. X. & H. F.: 102
World market leaders: 98

DER SCHWARZWALD EINMAL ANDERS BETRACHTET
A NEW WAY OF LOOKING AT THE BLACK FOREST

von oben / from above

im Profil / in profile

die Bewohner / the inhabitants

die Fakten / the facts

Der Schwarzwald ist bekannt für dunkle Wälder und grüne Wiesen, Berge und Täler, Kirschtorten und Kuckucksuhren. Er ist die Heimat von Weltmeistern, Weltmarktführern und dem weltberühmten Bollenhut. Es gibt 24.000 Kilometer markierte Wanderwege, 1.700 Narrenzünfte und über 20 Sterne-Restaurants – so viele wie in keiner anderen Region Deutschlands. Hier gibt es Hinterwälder Kühe, Schwarzwälder Füchse und den Badischen Riesenregenwurm, der nirgendwo sonst vorkommt. Und es gibt Schwarzwälderinnen und Schwarzwälder, die die Landschaft seit Jahrhunderten prägen und von ihr geprägt sind.

„Total alles über den Schwarzwald" stellt diese ebenso sympathische wie vielfältige Region in all ihren Facetten vor.

Der geografische Schwarzwald ist etwa 160 km lang und 60 km breit. Streng genommen gehören Karlsruhe und Lörrach, Breisach und Badenweiler, der Europa-Park und der Kaiserstuhl also gar nicht dazu. Selbst Freiburg, für viele die Hauptstadt des Schwarzwalds, liegt eigentlich nicht im Schwarzwald, sondern im Breisgau. Aber weil wir all diese schönen Orte nicht unerwähnt lassen wollen, meinen wir immer die Ferienregion Schwarzwald, wenn wir vom Schwarzwald sprechen.

Viel Vergnügen.

The Black Forest is known for dark woods and green meadows, mountains and valleys, cherry cakes and cuckoo clocks. It is home to world champions, world market leaders and the world-famous Bollenhut hat. The region boasts 24,000 kilometres of marked hiking trails, 1,700 fools' guilds and over 20 starred restaurants – more than any other region in Germany. Its native animals include Hinterwälder Cattle, Black Forest Horses and the Baden Giant Earthworm, which is found nowhere else in the world. And then there are the Black Forest women and men who have been shaping this landscape for centuries and have in turn been shaped by it.

"The Complete Black Forest" presents this congenial and diverse region in all its many facets.

In geographic terms, the Black Forest is about 160 km wide and 60 km long. Strictly speaking, Karlsruhe and Lörrach, Breisach and Badenweiler, the Europa-Park and the Kaiserstuhl are not really part of this region. Even Freiburg, which many people consider the capital of the Black Forest, is in fact not in the Black Forest but in Breisgau instead. But because we did not want to leave out all these beautiful places, when we speak here of the Black Forest we always mean the Black Forest as a holiday destination.

Enjoy!

Die Autoren / The authors
Die Gestalterinnen / The graphic designers

Wälder und Täler, Flüsse und Städte
Forests and valleys, rivers and cities

Der Schwarzwald ist das größte und höchste zusammenhängende Mittelgebirge Deutschlands. Die gesamte Ferienregion Schwarzwald ist knapp 200 km lang und bis zu 90 km breit. / The true Black Forest in the strict sense is the largest and highest continuous low mountain range in Germany. But the Black Forest considered as a holiday region covers an area of nearly 200 by 90 km.

WO SICH SCHWARZWÄLDER NIEDERGELASSEN HABEN
WHERE PEOPLE FROM THE BLACK FOREST HAVE SETTLED

Zell, Weingarten & New Offenburg
Drei Streusiedlungen in Ste. Genevieve County, Missouri, 120 km südwestlich von St. Louis
Three scattered settlements in Ste. Genevieve County, Missouri, 120 km southwest of St. Louis

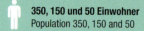

350, 150 und 50 Einwohner
Population 350, 150 and 50

~ 1830
Von Auswanderern aus dem Schwarzwald gegründet
Founded by emigrants from the Black Forest

In New Offenburg wird bis heute Englisch und Alemannisch gesprochen.
Both English and Alemannic are still spoken in New Offenburg today.

Black Forest Inn, Minneapolis, Minnesota

Black Forest Inn, Stanhope, New Jersey

Café Schwarzwald, Calvià-Peguera, Madeira

Colonia Tovar, Venezuela
70 km westlich von Caracas
70 km west of Caracas

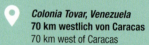

~ 20.000 Einwohner
Population ca. 20,000

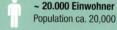

Gegründet von 400 Kaiserstühlern, die 1842 nach Südamerika auswanderten
Founded by 400 people from Kaiserstuhl who emigrated to South America in 1842

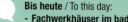

Bis heute / To this day:
- Fachwerkhäuser im badischen Stil
  Baden-style half-timbered houses
- Alemannischer Dialekt (Alemán Coloniero)
  Alemannic dialect (Alemán Coloniero)
- Alemannische Fasnet
  Alemannic carnival
- Schwarzwälder Kirschtorte
  Black Forest Cake
- Kuckucksuhren
  Cuckoo clocks
- Schäufele u.v.a.
  Pork shoulder and other traditional dishes

Ein Wald voller Farben
A colourful forest

Die Farben des Schwarzwalds, die jeder kennt
The colours of the Black Forest that everyone knows

SC Freiburg
football club

UHU
glue

Bollenhut
traditional hat

Rothaus Tannenzäpfle
beer

Duravit
bathroom fittings

Schwarzwälder Kirschtorte
Black Forest Cake

Schwarzwälder Schinken
Black Forest Ham

Schwarzwaldverein
Black Forest Hiking Club

Karlsruher SC
football club

Schwarzwälder Fuchs
Black Forest Horse

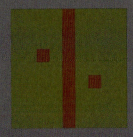

Tanne
fir tree

Hinterwälder Rind
Hinterwald cattle

hansgrohe
bathroom fittings

Dual
audio and video electronics

Lange Rote (Bratwurst am Freiburger Münstermarkt)
sausage at the cathedral market in Freiburg

Fischer Dübel
screw anchors

Südlicher Schwarzwald
Southern Black Forest

Kuckucksuhr
cuckoo clock

Freiburger Münster
Freiburg Cathedral

Nördlicher Schwarzwald
Northern Black Forest

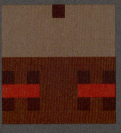

Vogtsbauernhof
open-air museum

Gipfelstürmer
Peak performers

Die Berge des Schwarzwalds
The mountains of the Black Forest

DIE HÖCHSTEN / THE HIGHEST

FELDBERG	BALDENWEGER BUCK	SEEBUCK	HERZOGENHORN	BELCHEN
1.493 m	1.460 m	1.448 m	1.415 m	1.414 m

FELDBERGMASSIV / FELDBERG RANGE

Höchster Berg Baden-Württembergs. Höchste Erhebung aller deutschen Mittelgebirge Deutschlands. Höchster Berg Deutschlands außerhalb der Alpen.
Highest mountain in Baden-Württemberg. Highest elevation of all German low mountain ranges. Highest mountain in Germany outside the Alps.

Liegt neben dem Feldberg und wird meist übersehen
Located next to the Feldberg and usually overlooked

Mit Feldbergturm, Schinkenmuseum und einem Trauzimmer
With Feldberg Tower, Ham Museum and a wedding room

Im Olympiastützpunkt auf 1.300 m trainieren Gewichtheber, Judoka, Leichtathleten, Mountainbiker, Ruderer, Fechter, Tennisspieler, Boxer, Ringer, Langläufer, Nordische Kombinierer u. v. a.
Weightlifters, judokas, track and field athletes, mountain bikers, rowers, fencers, tennis players, boxers, wrestlers, cross-country skiers, Nordic combiners and many others train at the Olympic base at 1,300 m.

Bildet mit dem Schweizer, Elsässer, Großen und Kleinen Belchen das Belchen-System. Belchen, keltisch: der Strahlende
Together with the Swiss, Alsatian, Big and Small Belchen forms the Belchen System. Belchen is Celtic for "the radiant one".

102
Berge / mountains
1.000–1.493 m
Höhe / elevation

DIE SCHÖNSTEN NAMEN
THE LOVELIEST NAMES

SCHAUINSLAND
1.284 m

Freiburgs Hausberg
Freiburg's local mountain

GSCHEIDKOPF
1.064 m

Darf auch von Dummköpfen bestiegen werden.
Means "clever head" but can also be climbed by thickheads.

MERKUR
668 m

Hausberg Baden-Badens, benannt nach dem römischen Götterboten
Baden-Baden's local mountain, named after Mercury, the Roman messenger of the gods

KAISERSTUHL
557 m

Verdankt seinen Namen dem Fürstengericht, das König Otto III. im Jahr 994 hier abhielt
Owes its name to the royal court King Otto III held here in 994

YBERG
515 m

Der Name stammt von „Iwa" ab, altdeutsch: Eibe.
The name derives from "Iwa", old German for yew.

DIE SCHAUERLICHSTEN NAMEN
THE SCARIEST NAMES

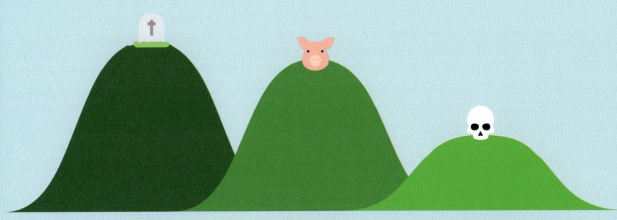

TOTE MANN
1.320 m

(auch Toter Mann)
Hausberg von Oberried
(aka "Toter Mann" = Dead Man)
Oberried's local mountain

SCHWEINEKOPF
1.257 m

Liegt bei Präg.
Lit. Pig's Head, located near Präg

TOTENKOPF
557 m

Berg im Kaiserstuhl. Verdankt seinen Namen den Hinrichtungen, die König Otto III. im Jahr 994 hier vollstrecken ließ.
Mountain in the Kaiserstuhl. It gets its name (lit. Skull Mountain) from the executions that King Otto III had carried out here in 994.

Wasser im Überfluss
Water, water everywhere

Die Gewässer des Schwarzwalds / The waters of the Black Forest

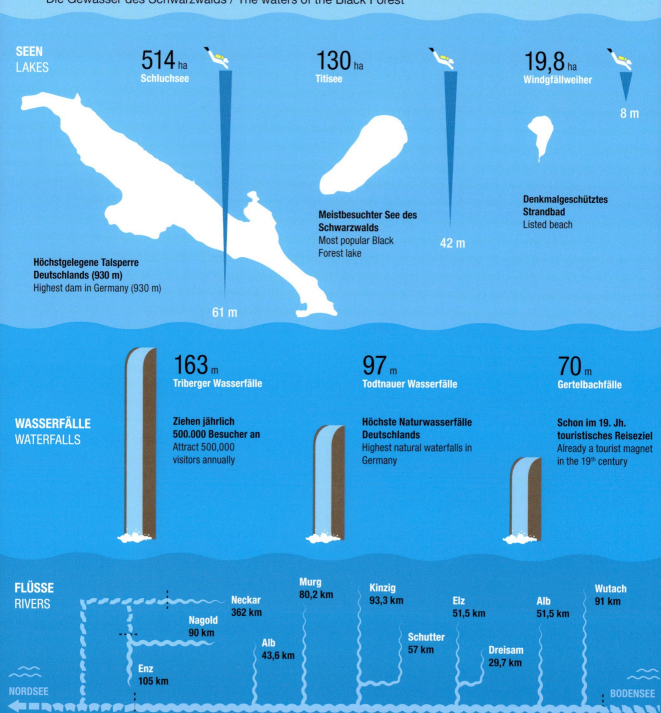

17 Thermen / thermal baths
Im Schwarzwald baden
Bathing in the Black Forest

 10 Mineralwässer / mineral waters
Den Schwarzwald trinken
Drinking the Black Forest

 10 Schnapsbrunnen / schnapps fountains
In Sasbachwalden Schnaps probieren und das Geld in ein Kästchen legen
In Sasbachwalden you can sample schnapps and just put money in a box.

9,75 ha Feldsee — 32 m
Größter Karsee des Schwarzwalds
Largest tarn in the Black Forest

6 ha Schlüchtsee — 5 m
1791 als Eissee für die Brauerei Rothaus aufgestaut.
Dammed in 1791 as an ice lake for the Rothaus brewery

3,7 ha Mummelsee — 18 m
Im See leben keine Fische. Aber Nixen.
There are no fish in the lake. But there are mermaids.

3,1 ha Nonnenmattweiher — 7 m
War nach einem Dammbruch 1922 für 12 Jahre verschwunden.
Disappeared for 12 years after a dam burst in 1922.

2,7 ha Glaswaldsee — 11 m
Hier wurden Glasflaschen für Mineralwasser hergestellt.
Glass bottles for mineral water were once produced here.

66 m Allerheiligen-Wasserfälle
Größte natürliche Wasserfälle des Mittleren Schwarzwalds
Largest natural waterfalls in the Central Black Forest

40 m Zweribach-Wasserfälle
Liegen in einem der ältesten Naturwaldreservate Deutschlands.
Located in one of Germany's oldest natural forest reserves

40 m Todtmooser Wasserfall
Offizielles flächenhaftes Naturdenkmal aufgrund von „Seltenheit nach Gestalt, Größe und Standort im Ortsbereich"
Official natural monument due to "rarity in form, size and setting in the local area"

6 m Geroldsauer Wasserfall
In den 1960ern wurden Rhododendronbüsche angepflanzt.
Rhododendrons were planted here in the 1960s.

Brigach 40,4 km
Breg 46,1 km
Donauquelle / Source of the Danube
Donau / Danube 2.840 km
SCHWARZES MEER / BLACK SEA

Nordschwaben, Kleinkanada und Palmspring
Northern Swabia, Little Canada and Palm Springs

Sie alle liegen im Schwarzwald. Aha! Auf dieser zauberhaften Insel haben viele Dörfer, Berge, Täler und Flüsse sehr (an)sprechende Namen. / The Black Forest is like an enchanting island where many of the villages, mountains, valleys and rivers bear funny and revealing names.

Französischer Ozean / French Ocean

Munitionstransporter / Ammunition ship
„Schwarzwald A1400"
1955 gebaut in der Werft Ateliers et Chantiers de Bretagne; 1959 gekauft vom Bundesverteidigungsministerium; 1961–1974 im Einsatz für das 2. Versorgungsbatallion Nordsee. „Bordhund Blacky neigt zu Seekrankheit"; 1974 ausgemustert und an Griechenland verkauft. / 1955: built at the Ateliers et Chantiers de Bretagne shipyard; 1959: purchased by the German Ministry of Defence; 1961–1974: deployed in the 2nd North Sea supply battalion. Blacky, the ship's dog, is often seasick. 1974: decommissioned and sold to Greece.

Dampfschiff / Steamship
„Schwarzwald"
1911 gebaut in den Schichau-Werken Elbing (heute: Elbląg, Polen); 1912 Erstfahrt nach Südamerika; 1917 vor Borkum gesunken / 1911: built at the Schichau shipyard in Elbing (today Elbląg, Poland); 1912: maiden voyage to South America; 1917: sunk off Borkum

Map

A fictional map with German place names on an island surrounded by the Helvetische See / Helvetian Sea (south) and Schwäbische See / Swabian Sea (east).

Compass: N, O, S, W

Main marked locations (⊚):
- Kleinkanada
- Zuflucht
- Palmspring
- Aha

Settlements (north to south):
- Gottesaue
- Muggensturm
- Teufelsmühle
- Igelsloch
- Siehdichfür
- Umweg
- Nonnenmiß
- Poppeltal
- In der Höll
- Allerheiligen
- Freudenstadt
- Schopfloch
- Romsgrund
- Vierundzwanzig
- Höfe
- Bettenhausen
- Busenweiler
- Vorderlehengericht
- Höllgraben
- Bösingen
- Sexau
- Hexenloch
- Himmelreich
- Hexental
- Holzarbeit
- Toter Mann
- Neubierhäusle
- Sumpfohren
- Schauinsland
- Notschrei
- Heitersheim
- Vorderes Elend
- Muggenbrunn
- Aftersteg
- Fahl
- Wutach
- Müllheim
- Holzinshaus
- Faulenfürst
- Käsacker
- Blasiwald
- Schlechtbach
- Finsterlingen
- Schweigmatt
- Hühner
- Nordschwaben
- Küssaberg

Peaks (▲):
- Mörderdobel
- Oberer Hundskopf
- Am Schwitzberg
- Tochtermannsberg
- Biereck
- Ochsenkopf
- Totenkopf
- Herzogenhorn
- Schweinekopf

Rivers:
- Wolf
- Dreisam
- Klemmbach
- Wiese

Alemannisch schmeckt nach Bauernbrot und Landluft*
Alemannic tastes of farmhouse bread and country air*

* frei nach / loosely based on **Ernst Bloch**.

Im größten Teil des Schwarzwalds wird Alemannisch gesprochen, oder, wie die Einheimischen sagen, „Schwarzwälderisch". Im nordöstlichen Teil spricht man Schwäbisch. / The Alemannic dialect is spoken throughout most of the Black Forest. The locals call it "Schwarzwälderisch". In the northeast people speak the Swabian dialect.

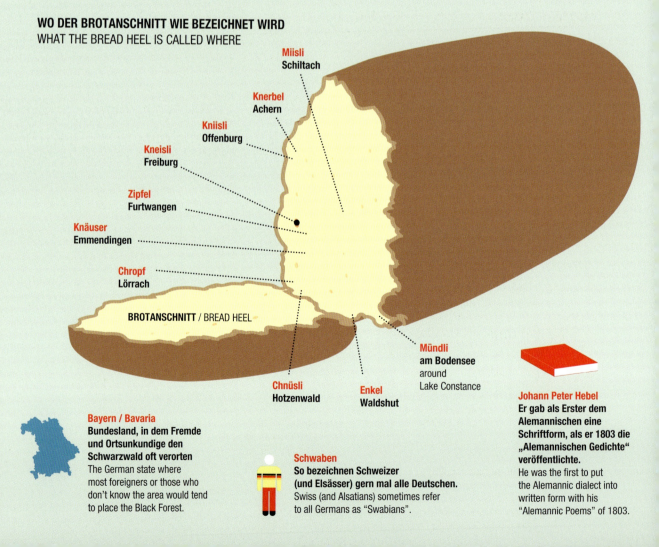

WO DER BROTANSCHNITT WIE BEZEICHNET WIRD
WHAT THE BREAD HEEL IS CALLED WHERE

- **Miisli** Schiltach
- **Knerbel** Achern
- **Kniisli** Offenburg
- **Kneisli** Freiburg
- **Zipfel** Furtwangen
- **Knäuser** Emmendingen
- **Chropf** Lörrach
- **Chnüsli** Hotzenwald
- **Enkel** Waldshut
- **Mündli** am Bodensee / around Lake Constance

BROTANSCHNITT / BREAD HEEL

Bayern / Bavaria
Bundesland, in dem Fremde und Ortsunkundige den Schwarzwald oft verorten
The German state where most foreigners or those who don't know the area would tend to place the Black Forest.

Schwaben
So bezeichnen Schweizer (und Elsässer) gern mal alle Deutschen.
Swiss (and Alsatians) sometimes refer to all Germans as "Swabians".

Johann Peter Hebel
Er gab als Erster dem Alemannischen eine Schriftform, als er 1803 die „Alemannischen Gedichte" veröffentlichte.
He was the first to put the Alemannic dialect into written form with his "Alemannic Poems" of 1803.

Wort	Deutsch	English
aacho	ankommen	arrive
allewiil	manchmal	sometimes
Bäpp	Klebstoff	adhesive
Bäpper	Sticker	sticker
bappig	klebrig	sticky
bätschnass	klatschnass	soaking wet
Bibbeleskäs	Quark	curd cheese
bicklhart	sehr hart	very hard
bigoscht	wahrlich	truly
Brägele	Bratkartoffeln	fried potatoes
bressiere	drängeln	jostle
chalt	kalt	cold
Chind	Kind	child
desell	jener (Herr) dort	that (man) there
disell	jene (Dame) dort	that (woman) there
Dubel	Depp	git
Dunschtig	Donnerstag	Thursday
ebbis	etwas	a bit
Giggel	Huhn	chicken
Götte	Taufpate	godfather
Guzle	Bonbon	sweet
Hag	Zaun	fence
Hagseicher	Idiot	idiot
Häs	Kleidung	clothing
hebe	halten	hold
Heugumber	Heuschrecke	locust
hii	kaputt	broken
hitt	heute	today
jucke	springen	jump
käb	knapp	scarce
Krummbeere	Kartoffel	potato
Krutzele	Stachelbeere	gooseberry
Lalli	Zunge	tongue
Moris	Angst	fear
müpfe	meckern	complain
nakeie	hinfallen	fall down
nümme	nicht mehr	no longer
Pfnüsel	Schnupfen	sniffles
pfnuuse	schlafen	sleep
Ranzepfiife	Bauchweh	stomachache
Rotzlumpe	Taschentuch	handkerchief
Schdiege	Treppe	stairs
Schlotzer	Lutscher	lolly
Schmutz	Fett	fat
Schnurre	Mund	mouth
Schoofseckel	sehr unsympathischer Mensch	very disagreeable person
seggle	rennen	run
sellmol	damals	back then
Siëch	Schlitzohr	rascal
Suublotere	Schweinsblase	pig's bladder
Tschooli	guter Zeitgenosse mit Eselsgeduld	sweet-natured person, dupe
uselampe	heraushängen	hang out
verseggle	irreführen, (beim Fußball) umdribbeln	mislead, feint (in football)
zuelose	zuhören	listen

Wie heißen Sie?
What's your name?

Typische Schwarzwälder Familiennamen
Typical Black Forest surnames

KIENZLER	Beha	Brinkmann / Mehnert-Brinkmann
Schweizer / Münzer	Grieshaber	Engesser
ISELE	Matt	Dörflinger
Weißhaar	Morath	KLAUSMANN
Ketterer	Hettich	Asal
Jehle	Kimmig	Jäckle / Knöpfle
Gut / Hirt	Strittmatter	Faller
Rotzinger	Winterhalder / Bächle	Allgaier
Marder / Haberstroh	Bürklin	Blaich
Dold	Joos	Waldvogel / Finkbeiner

Schneller, höher, weiter
Faster, higher, further

Der superduperlative Schwarzwald / Black Forest superduperlatives

18 cm
KLEINSTES ALPHORN DER WELT
WORLD'S SMALLEST ALPHORN
Franz Schüssele aus Friesenheim
Franz Schüssele from Friesenheim

KLEINSTER KIRCHTURM DER WELT
WORLD'S SMALLEST CHURCH SPIRE
Evangelische Versöhnungskirche
Marbach/Villingen-Schwenningen
3,8 m

2.500 Plätze / seats
GRÖSSTES OPERNHAUS DEUTSCHLANDS
GERMANY'S LARGEST OPERA HOUSE
Festspielhaus Baden-Baden

ÄLTESTER GASTHOF DEUTSCHLANDS
GERMANY'S OLDEST INN
Zum Roten Bären, Freiburg
Über / Over 700 Jahre alt / years old

29 Forellen-Gerichte / trout dishes
GRÖSSTE FORELLEN-SPEISEKARTE BADEN-WÜRTTEMBERGS
MOST EXTENSIVE TROUT MENU IN BADEN-WÜRTTEMBERG
Schwarzwaldgasthof Tannenmühle, Grafenhausen

knapp / just under 100 Einwohner inhabitants
KLEINSTE GEMEINDE BADEN-WÜRTTEMBERGS
SMALLEST MUNICIPALITY IN BADEN-WÜRTTEMBERG
Böllen

1.000 m
HÖCHSTGELEGENE BRAUEREI DEUTSCHLANDS
HIGHEST-ALTITUDE BREWERY IN GERMANY
Badische Staatsbrauerei Rothaus

GRÖßTER MARKTPLATZ DEUTSCHLANDS
GERMANY'S LARGEST MARKET SQUARE
Freudenstadt
Ursprünglich sollte hier ein Schloss gebaut werden.
Originally a palace was meant to be built here.

EINER DER HÖCHSTPRÄMIERTEN WEINORTE DEUTSCHLANDS
ONE OF GERMANY'S TOP WINE-GROWING VILLAGES
Durbach

LÄNGSTE BANKLIEGE DER WELT
WORLD'S LONGEST BENCH
Todtnauberg
44 m

ÄLTESTE STADT BADEN-WÜRTTEMBERGS
OLDEST TOWN IN BADEN-WÜRTTEMBERG
Rottweil
74 n. Chr. / AD

GRÖßTER HOLZFASSKELLER DEUTSCHLANDS
BIGGEST WINE CELLAR WITH WOODEN BARRELS IN GERMANY
Badischer Winzerkeller, Breisach am Rhein

GRÖßTES ADVENTSKALENDERHAUS DER WELT
WORLD'S LARGEST ADVENT CALENDAR HOUSE
Gengenbacher Rathaus
Gengenbach town hall

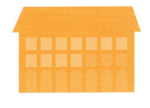

KLEINSTES STANDESAMT DEUTSCHLANDS
GERMANY'S SMALLEST CIVIL REGISTRY OFFICE
Triberg
1,5 m²

1. E-MAIL DEUTSCHLANDS
GERMANY'S 1ST EMAIL
Ging am 2.8.1984 auf einem Server der Universität Karlsruhe ein.
Received on a server at the University of Karlsruhe on 2 August 1984.

WÄRMSTER ORT DEUTSCHLANDS
WARMEST PLACE IN GERMANY
Ihringen am Kaiserstuhl

* jährliche Durchschnittstemperatur
annual average temperature

>12° C*

LÄNGSTE GEDECKTE HOLZBRÜCKE EUROPAS
EUROPE'S LONGEST COVERED WOODEN BRIDGE
Bad Säckingen
203,13 m

GRÖßTES WC DER WELT
WORLD'S LARGEST WC
Duravit Besucher-Center, Hornberg
7 m

Im 18. Jahrhundert erbaut
Built in the 18th century

Natur pur
Nature at its best

Im Schwarzwald wird die Natur umfangreich geschützt.
Nature conservation is a top priority in the Black Forest.

SCHONWÄLDER
PROTECTED FORESTS
11.569 ha

Geschützte Waldgebiete mit eingeschränkter wirtschaftlicher Nutzung
Protected forest areas with restricted economic use

LANDSCHAFTSSCHUTZGEBIETE
LANDSCAPE PROTECTION AREAS
359.116 ha

Erhalten das Erscheinungsbild der Landschaft und dienen der Erholung
Protect cultural, managed landscapes and provide recreation areas

NATURSCHUTZGEBIETE
NATURE CONSERVATION AREAS
51.039 ha

Geschützte Natur und Landschaft zur Erhaltung, Entwicklung oder Wiederherstellung von Lebensstätten, Biotopen oder Lebensgemeinschaften bestimmter wild lebender Tier- und Pflanzenarten
Protect pristine natural landscapes in order to conserve, develop or restore habitats, biotopes or communities of certain species of wild fauna and flora

BANNWÄLDER
FOREST RESERVES
4.653 ha

Geschützte Waldgebiete, in denen keine Eingriffe oder Holzentnahme erlaubt sind
Protected forest areas where no interventions or timber extraction is permitted

Beispiele / Examples
Bärlochkar bei / near **Calw**, **Klebwald** im / in **Enzkreis**, **Schwarzahalden-Erweiterung** bei / near **Waldshut**

EINZELNE ODER FLÄCHENNATURDENKMÄLER
NATURAL MONUMENTS

Unter Naturschutz stehende bis zu 5 ha große Gebiete oder Einzelobjekte
Protected natural features or areas of up to 5 ha

Beispiele / Examples
Ellbachsee bei / near **Baiersbronn**, **Bernsteinfels** bei / near **Gaggenau**, **Großvatertanne** am / on the shore of **Wilden See**

839
Flächennaturdenkmäler
natural monument areas
5.234 ha

3.338
Einzelobjekte
natural features
5,17 ha

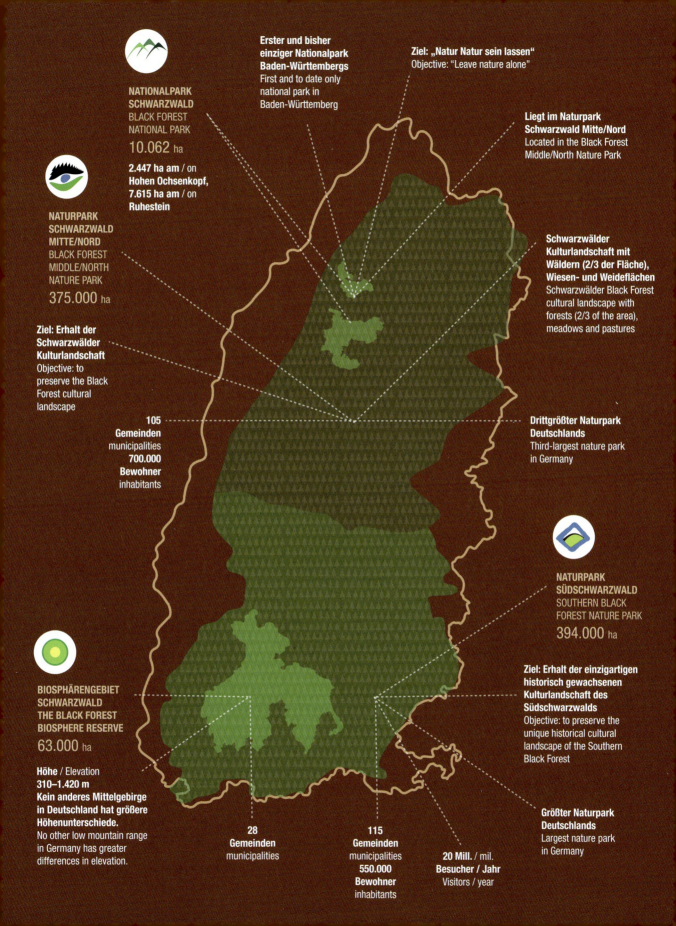

Den Wald vor lauter Bäumen
Can't see the forest for the trees

Warum der Schwarzwald Schwarzwald heißt.
Why is it called the Black Forest?

BAUMARTEN (IM KÖRPERSCHAFTS- UND STAATSWALD)
TREE SPECIES (IN CORPORATE AND STATE FORESTS)

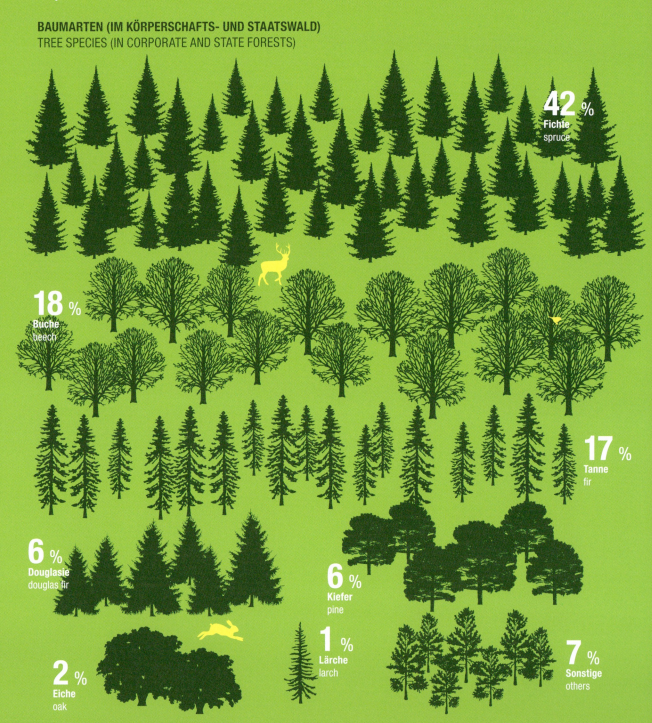

42 % Fichte / spruce
18 % Buche / beech
17 % Tanne / fir
6 % Douglasie / douglas fir
6 % Kiefer / pine
1 % Lärche / larch
2 % Eiche / oak
7 % Sonstige / others

FLÄCHE / AREA

460.000 ha

≈ **660.000 Fußballfelder** / football pitches

75 %

der Schwarzwald-Fläche ist bewaldet
of the land in the Black Forest is forested

WALDBESITZ / FOREST OWNERSHIP

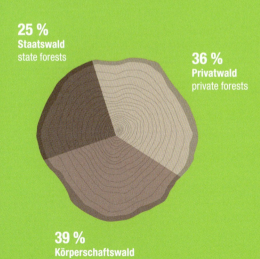

25 %
Staatswald
state forests

36 %
Privatwald
private forests

39 %
Körperschaftswald
(Städte und Gemeinden)
corporate forests
(towns and municipalities)

GESCHICHTE / HISTORY

Vor 10.000 Jahren: Steppe und Tundra
10,000 years ago: steppe and tundra

Mit der Erwärmung kommen Eschen, Eichen, Linden, Ulmen und Ahorn.
A warmer climate brings ash, oak, lime, elm and maple trees.

Vor 6.000 Jahren: Tannen, Buchen, Kiefern und Fichten kommen dazu.
6,000 years ago: firs, beeches, pines and spruces begin to thrive.

Die Römer nennen den dunklen Wald „silva nigra" = schwarzer Wald.
The Romans call the dark forest "silva nigra" = black forest.

Im „Hölzernen Zeitalter" (bis Mitte des 19. Jh.) wird fast alles aus Holz hergestellt. Das führt zu wirtschaftlichem Aufschwung des Schwarzwalds und zum Abholzen der Wälder.
In the "Wooden Age" (until the mid-19th century) almost everything is made of wood. This leads to an economic boom in the Black Forest but also to deforestation.

Die Folge: Im 18. Jh. ist der Schwarzwald beinahe verschwunden.
As a result, the Black Forest has almost disappeared by the 18th century.

1833 verabschiedet die Badische Regierung das erste Wiederaufforstungsgesetz zur Rettung des Schwarzwalds.
In 1833 the government in Baden passes the first reforestation act to save the Black Forest.

Ein Traum von Baum
Barking up the wrong tree

Tannen, Fichten und anderes Gehölz
Firs, spruces and other types of wood

Orte im Schwarzwald
BLACK FOREST TOWNS

Untersimonswald
Sasbachwalden
Harzhäusle   Schutterwald
Holz   Simonswald
Grünwald   Mooswald
Vordersteinwald
Holzhäusle   Holzschlag
Burg am Wald
Waldachtal
Hölzlekönig   Kohlwald
Glaswald

GASTHAUSNAMEN IM SCHWARZWALD*
BLACK FOREST INN NAMES*

Drei Tannen   Haus Tanne
Schwarzwaldtanne   Tannenheim
Tannenblick
Grüne Tanne   Kaisers Tanne
Alte Tanne   Zur großen Tanne
Tannenhain   Tannen-Stube
Zur Tanne   Tannenmühle
Tannenhof

* Dem Autor ist im Schwarzwald kein nach der Fichte benanntes Gasthaus bekannt.
The author is not aware of any inn in the Black Forest with the word "Fichte" (spruce) in its name.

Fichtenzapfen
Spruce cone

Tannenzapfen
Fir cone

ZAPFENPFLÜCKER
CONE PICKER

Die Staatsklenge Nagold bietet eine einwöchige Ausbildung an.
The Staatsklenge Nagold forestry organisation offers a one-week training course.

JAGD / HUNTING

ca. 136.000 ha
Staatsjagdfläche / state-owned hunting grounds

davon / thereof

ca. 100.000 ha
Verwaltungsjagd
stewardship hunting grounds

ca. 36.000 ha
verpachtet
leased

dort jagen / hunting here are
ca. 1.400
revierlose Jäger
non-tenant hunters

SELTENER BAUM
SCHWARZWÄLDER HÖHENKIEFER
RARE TREE
BLACK FOREST PINE
Hochlagen des Nordschwarzwaldes
Higher altitudes in the Northern Black Forest
Kennzeichen: ausgesprochene Geradschaftigkeit
Characteristic: extremely straight trunk

51 m
HÖCHSTE TANNEN DEUTSCHLANDS
GERMANY'S TALLEST FIR TREE
Tannen bei Kälberbronn
Firs near Kälberbronn

> 67 m
+30 cm
Jahr / year
GRÖSSTER BAUM DEUTSCHLANDS
GERMANY'S TALLEST TREE
Douglasie Waldtraut im Freiburger Stadtwald, 1913 gepflanzt
Douglas fir named Waldtraut in Freiburg's municipal forest, planted in 1913

28,8 m³/ha
Totholzvorrat im gesamten baden-württembergischen Wald
Amount of deadwood in all forests in Baden-Württemberg

ca. 360 ha
SCHWEIZER WALD
SWISS FOREST
Wald bei Grafenhausen gehört seit 1530 dem Schweizer Kanton Schaffhausen.
The forest near Grafenhausen has belonged to the Swiss canton of Schaffhausen since 1530.

1 Schweizer Förster
Swiss forest ranger

Deutsche Waldarbeiter werden in Franken bezahlt.
German forest workers are paid in Swiss francs.

8.578 ha
GRÖSSTER STADTWALD DEUTSCHLANDS
GERMANY'S LARGEST MUNICIPAL FOREST
Baden-Baden

70 %
der Bäume im Nationalpark Schwarzwald sind Fichten.
of the trees in the Black Forest National Park are spruces.

Wenn aus Natur Kultur wird
When nature becomes culture

Holzwirtschaft / Timber industry

WO SCHWARZWÄLDER HOLZ ZUM EINSATZ KOMMT
WHERE BLACK FOREST WOOD IS USED

1715
wurden außer Landes geflößt:
the following were rafted out of the province:

14.000
Holländerstämme
"Dutch logs"

51.000
Balken / beams

292.000
Dielen / planks

158.000
Latten / battens

Früher / Formerly

Räder Wheels
Eimer Pails
Besteck Kitchen utensils
Kämme Combs
Knöpfe Buttons
Butterfässer Butter churns

Im „Hölzernen Zeitalter" wird fast alles aus Holz hergestellt.
In the "Wooden Age", almost everything was made of wood.

Stühle Chairs
Flößerei Timber rafting
Schiffsbau Shipbuilding
Glasbläsereien Glass blowing
Bergbau Mining
Städtebau Urban construction
Amsterdam, Rotterdam ...
Köhlerei Charcoal burning

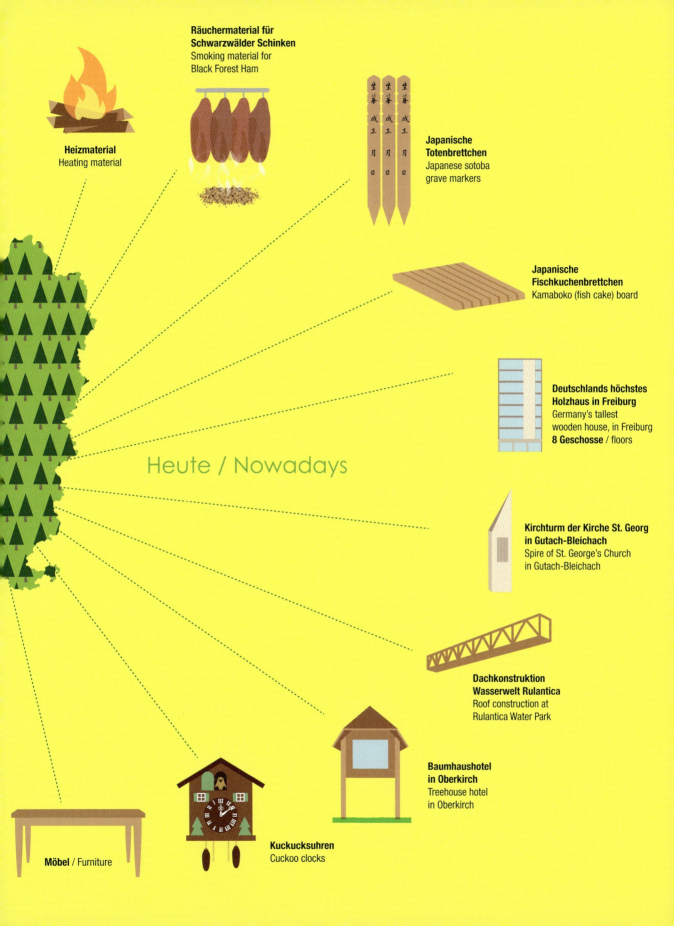

Wie spät ist es?
What time is it?

Eine Original Schwarzwälder Kuckucksuhr muss samt aller Einzelteile im Schwarzwald hergestellt worden sein. / In order to be considered an original Black Forest cuckoo clock, the clock and all its parts must be made in the Black Forest.

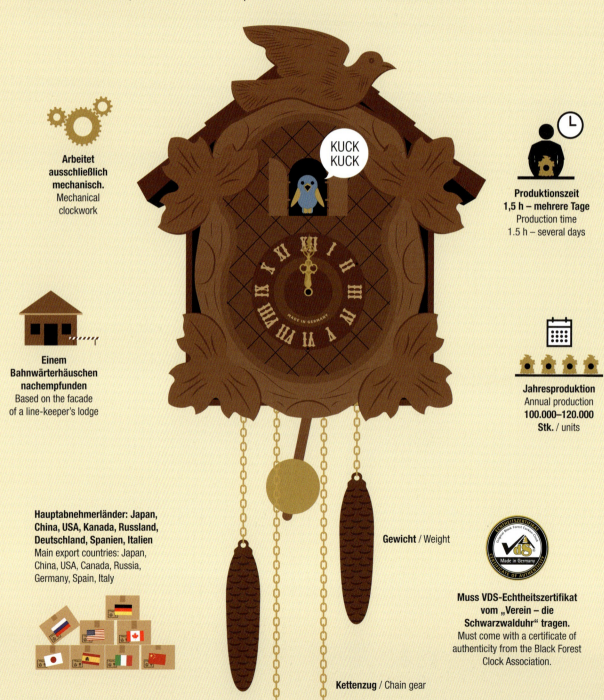

17. Jh. / 17th century
Italienische Händler bringen Uhren in den Schwarzwald. Dortige Handwerker bauen sie nach.
Italian merchants bring clocks to the Black Forest and local craftsmen make copies.

1850
Robert Gerwig, Direktor der Uhrmacherschule in Furtwangen, lobt Wettbewerb für eine zeitgemäße Uhr aus. Friedrich Eisenlohr reicht Bahnwärterhäuschen mit Zifferblatt ein.
Robert Gerwig, director of the Clockmaking School in Furtwangen, holds a competition for a modern clock. Friedrich Eisenlohr submits a design based on a line-keeper's lodge.

Uhrenträger tragen die einfachen Bauernuhren mit bemalten Metallplatten in die Welt hinaus. Die Schwarzwälder Uhrenindustrie entsteht.
Clock carriers take the simple peasant clocks with painted metal plates far beyond the region's borders. The Black Forest clock industry is born.

Geschichte / History

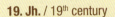

19. Jh. / 19th century
Industrialisierung setzt den kleinen Uhrmacherwerkstätten zu.
Industrialisation begins to crowd out the small watchmaking workshops.

1738
Franz Anton Ketterer aus Schönwald baut die erste Kuckucksuhr der Welt (nicht verbürgt).
Franz Anton Ketterer from Schönwald makes the world's first cuckoo clock (not documented).

1840
Ca. 1.000 Uhrmacher im Schwarzwald
approx. 1,000 clockmakers in the Black Forest

Die größte Kuckucksuhr der Welt
The world's biggest cuckoo clock

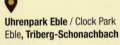 **Uhrenpark Eble** / Clock Park Eble, **Triberg-Schonachbach**

 Kuckuck / Cuckoo
4,5 m Länge / length
150 kg

Uhrwerk / Clockwork
4,5 x 4,5 m
6 t

Pendel / Pendulum
8 m

Die kleinste Kuckucksuhr der Welt
The world's smallest cuckoo clock

Höhe / Height
13,5 cm

Pendel / Pendulum
15 cm

 Uhrenmanufaktur Hubert Herr, Triberg

 1,4 kg

 Kuckuck / Cuckoo
5 cm

 Mechanisches Eintagewerk mit manueller Selbstabschaltung
Mechanical one-day clockwork with manual night shut-off

 Zeiger, Zifferblatt und Ziffern aus Holz
Wooden hands, dial and numbers

Das Markenzeichen
The trademark

Den Bollenhut gibt es eigentlich nur in drei Dörfern, im Schwarzwald insgesamt aber über 120 Trachten – Sebastian Wehrle setzt sie als Fotograf eindrücklich in Szene. / Originally, the Bollenhut actually is only worn in three villages, while the Black Forest has over 120 different folk costumes. Photographer Sebastian Wehrle strikingly stages them here.

Sehen kann man die Tracht
These costumes can be seen
Ostersonntag, Erntedankfest, Gemeindefeste, touristische Veranstaltungen, Schwarzwälder Freilichtmuseum Vogtsbauernhof in Gutach, Trachtenmuseum Haslach, Schwarzwaldmuseum in Triberg
Easter Sunday, harvest festivals, community festivals, tourist events, Vogtsbauernhof Black Forest Open Air Museum in Gutach, Black Forest Costume Museum in Haslach, Black Forest Museum in Triberg

Schwarzer Hut
Black hat

Schwarze, rot gefütterte Jacke
Black jacket with red lining

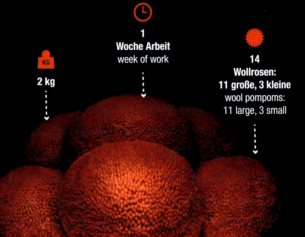

7.1.1797
Herzog Friedrich Eugen von Württemberg verordnet für seine Schwarzwald-Gemeinden, Strohhüte müssen die „übliche Dekoration von schwarzer und roter Farbe" tragen.
Duke Friedrich Eugen von Württemberg decrees that straw hats worn in the Black Forest communities under his rule must bear the "usual decoration in black and red".

Die ersten Hüte haben nur aufgemalte Kreise.
In the early hats the circles were painted on.

20 Jahre später kommen die flauschigen Woll-Bollen dazu.
20 years later the fluffy pompoms were added.

International bekannt wird der Bollenhut 1950 durch den Film „Schwarzwaldmädel".
The Bollenhut rose to international fame through the 1950 film "The Black Forest Girl".

2 kg

1 Woche Arbeit
week of work

14 Wollrosen: 11 große, 3 kleine
wool pompoms: 11 large, 3 small

Schwarz, wenn verheiratet
Black when married

Darf nur in den protestantischen Orten Gutach, Kirnbach, Reichenbach im Mittleren Schwarzwald getragen werden
May only be worn in the Protestant towns of Gutach, Kirnbach and Reichenbach in the Central Black Forest

Wird trotzdem überall getragen
Are nevertheless worn everywhere

Kragen, bestickt mit Flitterzeug
Collar embroidered with rhinestones

Goller
Partlet

Weißes Hemd mit Puffärmeln
White blouse with puff sleeves

Samtmieder mit eingestickten Blümchen
Velvet bodice embroidered with flowers

Schwarzer Wiefelrock
Black skirt

Alles unter einem Dach
Everything under one roof

Schwarzwaldhäuser sind Wohnstallhäuser mit weit heruntergezogenem Walmdach und schönen Namen. / Black Forest houses combine living quarters with stables under an extremely deep hipped roof and bear lovely names.

MODELL EINES SCHWARZWALDHAUSES VON FALLER
MODEL OF A BLACK FOREST FARM BY FALLER

Dach spendet im Sommer Schatten.
Deep eaves provide shade in summer.

Tiefer stehende Wintersonne kann Hauswand erwärmen.
The low winter sun can warm the walls of the house.

Krüppelwalmdach / Half-hipped roof
- mit Stroh, Schindeln oder Ziegeln gedeckt
  covered with thatch, shingles or bricks
- bietet geringe Angriffsfläche bei starkem Wind
  able to resist strong winds
- vermindert Schneelast
  steep slope reduces snow load

Das Dach wird von Holzsäulen getragen, die vom Boden bis zum First reichen.
The roof is supported by wooden columns reaching from the ground to the roof ridge.

Stall – Tiere lieferten früher Wärme für Wohnräume.
Stables – animals once supplied heat for the living spaces.

Küche und Stube mit Kachelofen
Kitchen and living room with cockle stove

Kühler Keller mit Lagerraum
Cool cellar with storage room

📍 **Im Schwarzwälder Freilichtmuseum Vogtsbauernhof kann man acht Höfe besichtigen.**
In the Black Forest Open Air Museum, eight farmsteads have been recreated for visitors.

Tenne mit Heu
Barn with hay

Balkon / Balcony

Holztreppe zur Eingangstü (auch bei viel Schnee zugänglich)
Wooden stairs up to the front door (accessible even in heavy snow)
Darunter häufig: Holzlager
Frequently with wood stored underneath

Briefträger im Schwarzwald müssen sich keine Straßennamen und Hausnummern merken, oft reicht der Hofname.
Postmen in the Black Forest don't have to remember street names and house numbers because often the name of the farm is enough.

Abrahambauer	Altrufehof	Ambsenhof	Auf den Höfen	Alter Rufenhof	Bäuerleshütte

Blumjockelesbauernhof

Behashof

Dürrhöfe	Großer Hof	Harzhäusle	Hasenhof	Hahnkrähenhof	Heidenbauernhof

Hinterbauernhof

Hof(bauernhof)

Höfenhof	Hutjörgenhof	Innere Höfe	Kappbläsihof	Kappenhof	Kappmathishof

Klausenhof

Klausbubenhof

Kohlenpeterhäusle	Küchlehof	Linkenbauernhof	Metzgerbauernhof	Platzhäusle	Raimartihof

Rufenhof

Schafmeiershof

Schniederlihof	Schuhhäusle	Schuhmächerlehof	Schuhmartishof	Schwabenhof	Singlerhof

Schneiderhäusle

Schottenhof

Stoffel(bauern)hof	Schweizerlehof	Theisenbläsishof	Tonisbauernhof	Thomalihof	Thumichelhof

Überhof

Urishof

Vierundzwanzighöfe	Vogelhäusle	Vorderbauernhof	Widiwandhof	Wirtshäusle

Die Kuh des Schwarzwalds
The cow of the Black Forest

Das robuste Hinterwälder Rind („Hirschvieh") hat sich an karge Böden und raues Klima angepasst. / The robust Hinterwald cattle breed has adapted to the poor soil and harsh climate of the Black Forest.

Wo Hinterwälder sonst noch leben
Where the Hinterwald breed can also be found

Arche Warder
Zoo Berlin
Zoom Erlebniswelt Gelsenkirchen
Minizoo Eickel, Herne
Zoo Duisburg
Thüringer Zoopark Erfurt
Tierpark Sommerhausen
Tierpark Walldorf
Wilhelma Stuttgart
Oberschwäbisches Museumsdorf Kürnbach, Bad Schussenried
Mainau-Bauernhof,
Farmyard, **Mainau im Bodensee**

Gute Zweinutzungsrasse: hohe Fleischqualität
Good dual-purpose breed producing high-quality meat

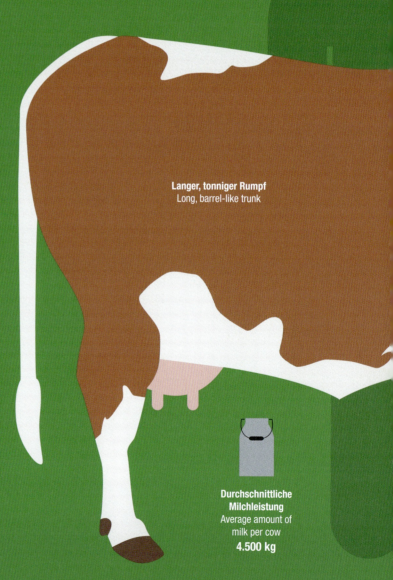

Langer, tonniger Rumpf
Long, barrel-like trunk

Durchschnittliche Milchleistung
Average amount of milk per cow
4.500 kg

700–800 kg ♂
380–420 kg ♀

Kleinste mitteleuropäische Rinderrasse / Smallest Central European cattle breed

Widerristhöhe / Withers height
130–135 cm ♂
118–122 cm ♀

Sehr langlebig und fruchtbar: bis zu 10 Kälber und mehr!
Extremely long-lived and fertile: up to 10 calves or more!

Gelb- bis Gelb-Rot-Schecken, weißer Kopf, Kopfabzeichen möglich
Pied coat in yellow to yellowish-red, white head, sometimes with facial markings

Wesentlich längerer Darm als andere Rassen
Much longer intestines than other breeds

Guter Futterverwerter
Efficient metabolism

Trittsicher, steigfähig, berggängig: an steile Hänge und lange Marschwege angepasst
Sure-footed and able to climb hills, negotiate steep pastures and endure long treks

Heimat: südlich des Feldbergs und des Belchen
Homeland: south of the Feldberg and Belchen peaks

Harte Klauen
Hard hooves

Es kreucht und fleucht
All creatures great and small ...

Es gibt Tiere. Und es gibt Tiere, die gibt es nur im Schwarzwald. / There are animals and there are animals. Some of them can only be found in the Black Forest.

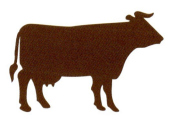

ca. 7.740
Vorderwälder Rind / Vorderwald Cattle

Hervorragend angepasst an Urgesteinsverwitterungsböden, steile Hanglagen, kurze Vegetationsdauer, raues Klima. Konstitutionsstabil, futterdankbar, weidetüchtig. Größer als die Hinterwälder Kuh.
Ideally adapted to rocky pastures, steep slopes, short vegetation periods and rough climates. Robust constitution, efficient feed converters, good grazers. Larger than Hinterwald Cattle.

ca. 2.320
Hinterwälder Rind / Hinterwald Cattle

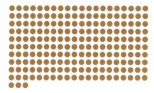

Mehr dazu S. 38
More on p. 38

1
Hirsch aus Bronze / Bronze stag

Steht im Höllental. Erinnert daran, dass ein Ritter der Burg Falkenstein einen prächtigen Hirsch erlegen wollte. In Todesangst sprang das Tier mit einem gewaltigen Satz über die Schlucht und entkam seinem Verfolger.
Stands in the Höllental Valley. Commemorates the tale of a knight from Falkenstein Castle who set out to slay a magnificent stag. At the last minute, the stag leapt across the wide gorge and escaped its pursuer.

700 (im Schwarzwald / in the Black Forest)
St. Märgener Fuchs / Black Forest Horse

(auch / aka: Schwarzwälder Kaltblut)
Farbe: Fuchs bis Dunkelfuchs, wenige Braune und Schimmel;
Fundament: korrekt, trocken, kräftige klare Gelenke, harte Hufe;
Eigenschaften: gutmütig, robust, anspruchslos, zugstark
Colour: pale to dark chestnut, more rarely brown and white;
Body: sturdy, trim, strong joints, hard hooves;
Properties: good-natured, robust, undemanding, good draft horse.

n^2-x
Badischer Riesenregenwurm
Lumbricus badensis

Endemit der natürlichen Fichtenwälder des Hochschwarzwaldes: Kommt weltweit nur zwischen Feldberg, Belchen und Wiesental oberhalb von 1.000 m vor.
Endemic to the natural spruce forests of the Upper Black Forest: Occurs worldwide only between Feldberg, Belchen and Wiesental above 1,000 m.

Eichhörnchen / Squirrel

Viele Schwarzwald-Gemeinden haben einen Eichhörnchenwald oder -park, wo man diese Tiere füttern kann.
Many Black Forest communities have a forest or park where visitors can feed the squirrels.

39
Zoos und Tierparks
Zoos and animal parks

Rottweiler

wurden im einst wichtigen Viehhandelszentrum Rottweil als Hüte- und Metzgerhunde eingesetzt.
were used as herding and butcher's dogs in Rottweil, once a major livestock trading post.

±0
Menschen haben diese Tiere in freier Wildbahn gesehen.
humans have seen these animals in the wild.

Wildkatze / Wild cat

Ähnelt der Hauskatze, ist mit ihr genetisch aber nicht verwandt.
Similar but not genetically related to the domestic cat.

Auerhuhn / Capercaillie

Größte Auerhuhnpopulation Zentraleuropas außerhalb der Alpen ≈ 300 Tiere
Largest capercaillie population in Central Europe outside the Alps ≈ 300 birds

Wolf / Wolf

Seit 2017 ist ein männlicher Wolf im Nordschwarzwald nachgewiesen.
A lone male wolf has been documented in the Northern Black Forest since 2017.

Luchs / Lynx

Hört Rascheln einer Maus in bis zu 50 m Entfernung.
Can hear the rustling of a mouse up to 50 m away.

43
Wildgehege
Game reserves

Häufig anzutreffen, vor allem auf den Speisekarten der Gasthäuser
Widespread, particularly on restaurant menus

Rotwild / Red deer **Rehwild** / Roe deer **Wildschwein** / Wild boar

Der Geschmack der Region
Regional flavour

Der Schwarzwälder ist ein Rohschinken und der berühmteste und beliebteste Schinken Deutschlands. / Black Forest Ham, a dry-cured smoked Ham, is Germany's most famous and beloved ham.

„Schwarzwälder Schinken" ist eine geschützte geografische Angabe (g.g.A.) der EU und darf nur im Schwarzwald produziert werden.
"Black Forest Ham" is a protected geographical indication (PGI) in the EU and may only be produced in the Black Forest.

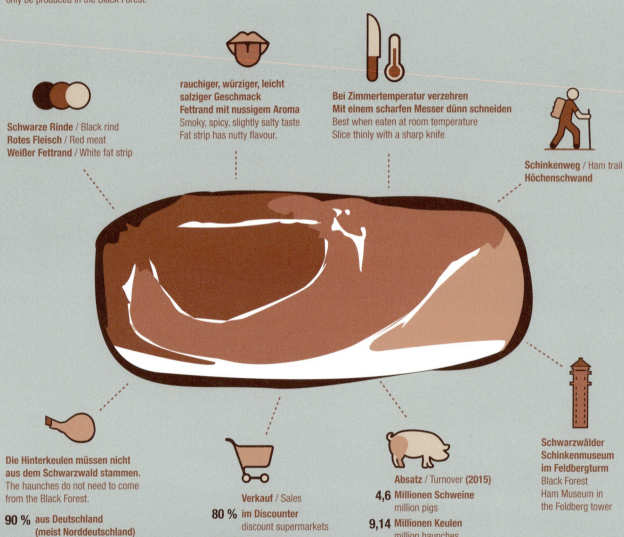

Schwarze Rinde / Black rind
Rotes Fleisch / Red meat
Weißer Fettrand / White fat strip

rauchiger, würziger, leicht salziger Geschmack
Fettrand mit nussigem Aroma
Smoky, spicy, slightly salty taste
Fat strip has nutty flavour.

Bei Zimmertemperatur verzehren
Mit einem scharfen Messer dünn schneiden
Best when eaten at room temperature
Slice thinly with a sharp knife

Schinkenweg / Ham trail
Höchenschwand

Die Hinterkeulen müssen nicht aus dem Schwarzwald stammen.
The haunches do not need to come from the Black Forest.

- **90 %** **aus Deutschland (meist Norddeutschland)** from Germany (primarily northern Germany)
- **10 %** **Ausland** from abroad

Verkauf / Sales
- **80 %** **im Discounter** discount supermarkets
- **10 %** **im Fachhandel** specialist shops
- **5 %** **in der Gastronomie** restaurants

Absatz / Turnover (2015)
- **4,6** **Millionen Schweine** million pigs
- **9,14** **Millionen Keulen** million haunches
- **50** **Millionen Kilo Fleisch** million kilos of meat

Schwarzwälder Schinkenmuseum im Feldbergturm
Black Forest Ham Museum in the Feldberg tower

AUSBEINEN / DEBONING HERSTELLUNG / PRODUCTION

Hinterkeule
Haunch

Knochen wird entfernt.
Bone is removed.

 7–10 kg

TROCKENPÖKELUNG / DRY-CURING (keine Injektion von Salzlake ins Fleisch / no brine injected into the meat)

Fleisch wird Wasser entzogen, Schinken ruht in Mutterlake.
Salt draws moisture from the meat and it rests in its own natural juices.

Salz, Pfeffer, Knoblauch, Koriander, Wacholderbeeren und andere Kräuter
Salt, pepper, garlic, coriander, juniper berries and other herbs

 2–3 Wochen / weeks
 5° C

BRENNEN / POST-SALTING

Macht typisch rote Farbe.
Creates the typical red colour.

Salz verteilt sich gleichmäßig im Schinken.
Salt distributes itself evenly throughout the ham.

 2 Wochen / weeks
 5° C

KALTRÄUCHERN / COLD-SMOKING

Macht dunkle äußere Farbe.
Creates the dark rind.

Mit Rauch heimischer Nadelhölzer und Sägespäne
Smoke from native conifers and sawdust

 2–3 Wochen / weeks
 max. 25° C

REIFEN / RIPENING

mind. / at least 25 %
Austrocknungsgrad
dehydration
2,2 : 1
Wasser-Eiweiß-Verhältnis
Water to protein ratio

 4–7 Wochen / weeks
 5° C
 5 kg

LAGERN / STORAGE

Vakuumverpackung, Leinenbeutel
Vacuum-packed, linen sack

 lange haltbar / long shelf life
 kühl, trocken / cool, dry

Die Torte zur Landschaft
The cake that put the Black Forest on the map

Eine Schwarzwälder Kirschtorte ist nicht leicht. Sie zu backen auch nicht. / Black Forest Cake is a rich dessert, with a history that's just as rich.

November 2007: Eine Studentin bewirft den damaligen baden-württembergischen Ministerpräsidenten Günther Oettinger mit einer Schwarzwälder Kirschtorte.
November 2007: A student throws a Black Forest Cake in the face of then Minister-President of Baden-Württemberg Günther Oettinger.

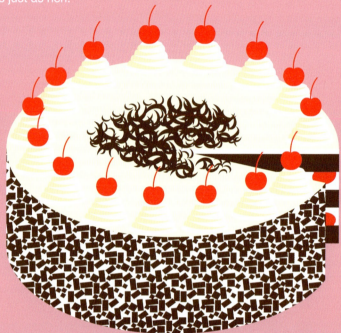

3,99 €
1 Torte (750 g), tiefgefroren, Edeka
1 private-label frozen cake (750 g) at the Edeka supermarket

9,99 €
1 Torte (1.400 g), tiefgefroren, Coppenrath & Wiese
1 frozen cake (1,400 g) from brand Coppenrath & Wiese

4,00 €
1 Stück, Konditorei Schäfer, Triberg
1 slice at Konditorei Schäfer, Triberg

ES GIBT AUCH SCHWARZWÄLDER KIRSCH-… / THERE ARE ALSO BLACK FOREST…

Eis
ice cream

Tiramisu
tiramisu

Muffins
muffins

Stollen-Bollenhut

Pralinen
pralines

Schokolade
chocolate

ZUTATEN / INGREDIENTS

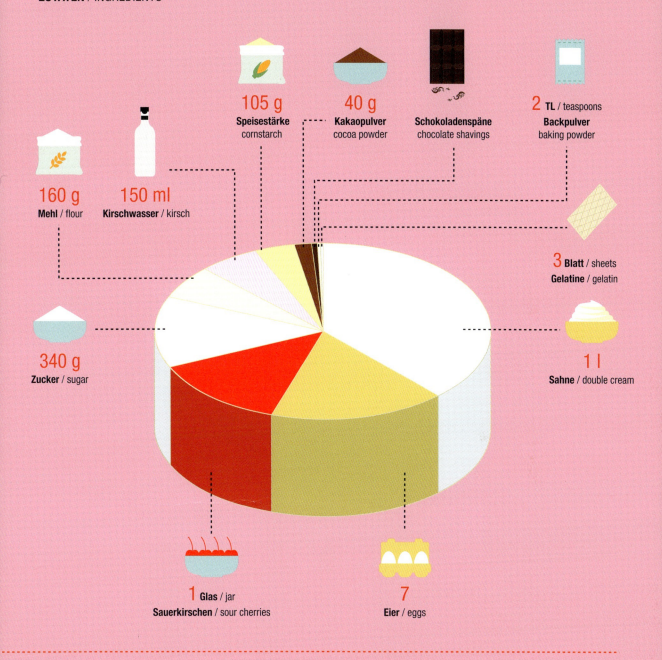

- **160 g** Mehl / flour
- **150 ml** Kirschwasser / kirsch
- **105 g** Speisestärke / cornstarch
- **40 g** Kakaopulver / cocoa powder
- Schokoladenspäne / chocolate shavings
- **2** TL / teaspoons Backpulver / baking powder
- **3** Blatt / sheets Gelatine / gelatin
- **1 l** Sahne / double cream
- **340 g** Zucker / sugar
- **1** Glas / jar Sauerkirschen / sour cherries
- **7** Eier / eggs

Fruchtaufstrich
fruit spread

Milchshakes
milkshakes

Bonbons
sweets

Halloren-Kugeln
Halloren-brand chocolate

… und Schwarzwälder
Kirsch-Kuchen
in der Dose!
… and Black Forest
cake in a tin!

Bier gibt Kraft
Beer fortifies and refreshes

Schwarzwälder Biere haben schöne Namen und markante Slogans. / Black Forest beers have creative names and distinctive slogans.

Jubelbier*
PRIVATBRAUEREI HOEPFNER
Karlsruhe

Badischer Rittertrunk
BRAUHAUS KÜHLER KRUG
Karlsruhe

Badisch Hell
BADISCH BRAUHAUS
Karlsruhe

„Ketterer sind netterer"
"Ketterer are better"
Black Forest Stout
FAMILIENBRAUEREI KETTERER
Hornberg

Dreisamhopfen
BRAUEREI GANTER
Freiburg

* Erstmals gebraut 1906 anlässlich der Goldenen Hochzeit von Großherzog Friedrich I. und seiner Frau Luise Marie Elisabeth. / First brewed in 1906 for the golden wedding anniversary of Grand Duke Frederick I and his wife, Luise Marie Elisabeth.

„Das Herzhopfen der Region"
"The hops at the heart of the region"
Black Forest Ale
BRAUEREI KETTERER
Pforzheim

Schwarzwald Weisse
PRIVATBRAUEREI WALDHAUS
Waldhaus

„Bierkultur seit 1283"
"Beer culture since 1283"
FÜRSTLICH FÜRSTENBERGISCHE BRAUEREI
Donaueschingen

„Aus der Region für die Region"
"From the region for the region"
HOCHDORFER KRONENBRAUEREI
Nagold-Hochdorf

„Erste Freiburger Gasthausbrauerei"
"First Freiburg brewery inside an inn"
MARTINSBRÄU
Freiburg

Dunkles Exportbier
HAUSBRÄU MÜLHAUPT
Lörrach-Brombach

Im Wein liegt Wahrheit
In vino veritas

In Wahrheit liegen die Anbaugebiete nicht im Schwarzwald, sondern in der „Ferienregion Schwarzwald". / And the truth is that the wine-growing regions are not actually located in the Black Forest proper but in the "Black Forest holiday region".

°Oe Ferdinand Oechsle aus Pforzheim erfand 1836 die Oechsle-Waage zur Bestimmung der Most-Dichte. Ferdinand Oechsle from Pforzheim invented the Oechsle scale for measuring the density of grape must in 1836.

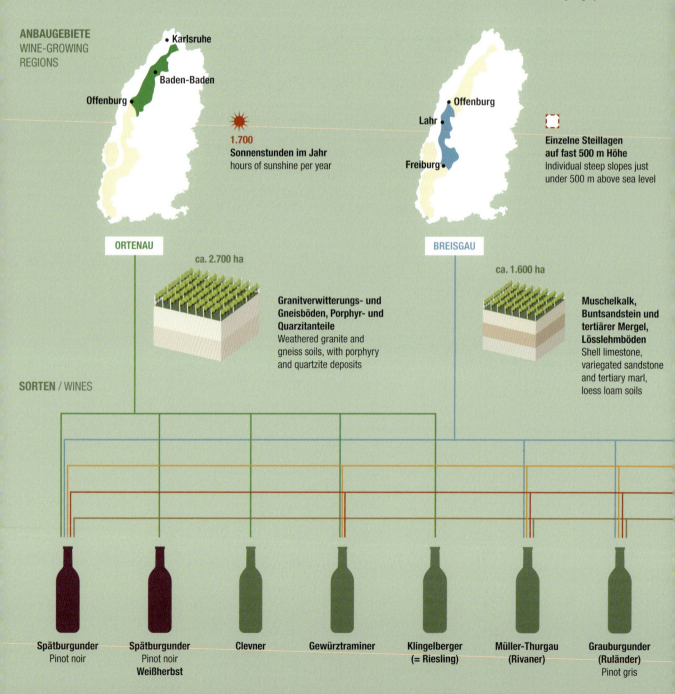

ANBAUGEBIETE / WINE-GROWING REGIONS

Karlsruhe, Baden-Baden, Offenburg

1.700 Sonnenstunden im Jahr / hours of sunshine per year

Offenburg, Lahr, Freiburg

Einzelne Steillagen auf fast 500 m Höhe / Individual steep slopes just under 500 m above sea level

ORTENAU — ca. 2.700 ha
Granitverwitterungs- und Gneisböden, Porphyr- und Quarzitanteile / Weathered granite and gneiss soils, with porphyry and quartzite deposits

BREISGAU — ca. 1.600 ha
Muschelkalk, Buntsandstein und tertiärer Mergel, Lösslehmböden / Shell limestone, variegated sandstone and tertiary marl, loess loam soils

SORTEN / WINES

- Spätburgunder / Pinot noir
- Spätburgunder / Pinot noir Weißherbst
- Clevner
- Gewürztraminer
- Klingelberger (= Riesling)
- Müller-Thurgau (Rivaner)
- Grauburgunder (Ruländer) / Pinot gris

Bocksbeutel
Bocksbeutel

Gibt es außerhalb Frankens nur im Baden-Badener Rebland.
Outside of Franken, this wine is produced only in the vineyards of Baden-Baden.

Die Flaschen heißen in Baden-Baden „Buddel".
In Baden-Baden the bottles are called "Buddel".

Das Oberrheinische Bäder- und Heimatmuseum in Bad Bellingen beherbergt die älteste Deutsche Rebordnung aus dem Jahr 1150. Darin wird geregelt, welcher Wein angebaut wird und wie viel die Bauern selbst behalten dürfen.
The Museum of Bathing Culture in the Upper Rhine Region in Bad Bellingen houses the oldest German wine-growing regulations, dating from 1150. They prescribe which wines can be grown and how much winegrowers are allowed to keep for themselves.

Sonnenreichste und wärmste Region Deutschlands
The sunniest and warmest region in Germany

1/3 aller Badischen Weine stammen von hier.
1/3 of all Baden wines come from here.

10 Kilometer langer, 120 m hoher Bergrücken südöstlich des Kaiserstuhls
10 km long, 120 m high mountain ridge southeast of Kaiserstuhl

Rechts des Oberrheins vom Grenzacher Horn bis Freiburg
On the right bank of the Upper Rhine, from the Grenzacher Horn to Freiburg

KAISERSTUHL — ca. 4.200 ha

TUNIBERG — ca. 1.000 ha

MARKGRÄFLER LAND — ca. 3.100 ha

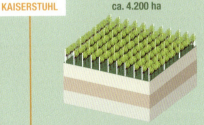

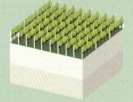

Terrassen, Löss- und Vulkanverwitterungsboden, vulkanisches Gestein
Terraces, loess and weathered volcanic soils, volcanic rock

Kalkgestein in Lössmantel
Limestone covered in loess soil

Lössschicht, tonige Lehm- und schwere Mergelböden, Urgestein
Loess layer, clayey loam and heavy marl soils, primary rock

Weißburgunder	Silvaner	Muskateller	Chardonnay	Sauvignon Blanc	Gutedel	Regent
Pinot blanc		Muscatel				

Dienst ist Dienst und Schnaps ist Schnaps
Work is work and liquor is liquor

Schwarzwälder Kirschwasser und andere Brände / There is a time and a place for everything – including Black Forest kirsch and other spirits

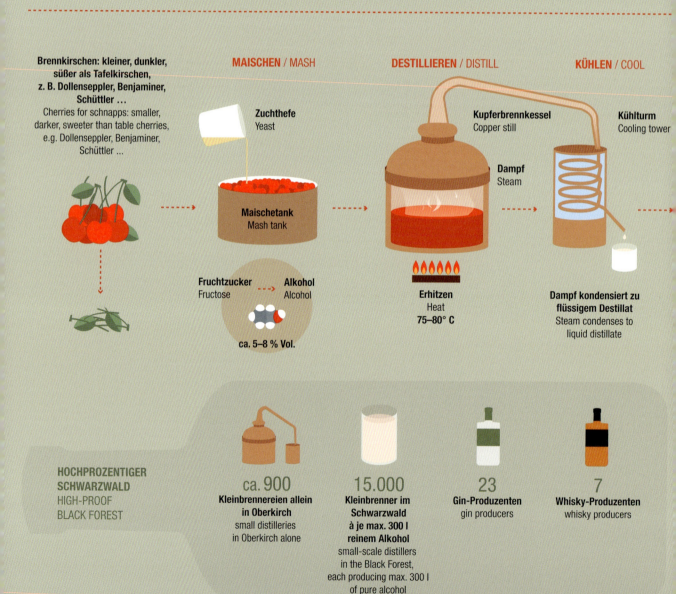

Brennkirschen: kleiner, dunkler, süßer als Tafelkirschen, z. B. Dollenseppler, Benjaminer, Schüttler …
Cherries for schnapps: smaller, darker, sweeter than table cherries, e.g. Dollenseppler, Benjaminer, Schüttler …

MAISCHEN / MASH
Zuchthefe / Yeast
Maischetank / Mash tank
Fruchtzucker / Fructose
Alkohol / Alcohol
ca. 5–8 % Vol.

DESTILLIEREN / DISTILL
Kupferbrennkessel / Copper still
Dampf / Steam
Erhitzen / Heat
75–80° C

KÜHLEN / COOL
Kühlturm / Cooling tower
Dampf kondensiert zu flüssigem Destillat
Steam condenses to liquid distillate

HOCHPROZENTIGER SCHWARZWALD
HIGH-PROOF BLACK FOREST

ca. 900 Kleinbrennereien allein in Oberkirch / small distilleries in Oberkirch alone

15.000 Kleinbrenner im Schwarzwald à je max. 300 l reinem Alkohol / small-scale distillers in the Black Forest, each producing max. 300 l of pure alcohol

23 Gin-Produzenten / gin producers

7 Whisky-Produzenten / whisky producers

Der berühmteste Schnaps des Schwarzwalds ist das Kirschwasser (auch „Schwarzwälder Kirsch" oder einfach „Kirsch"). / The most famous Black Forest schnapps is kirschwasser, also known simply as kirsch.

ANDERE SORTEN
OTHER VARIETIES

10 l Kirschen / cherries

1 l Kirschwasser / kirschwasser

Apfel, Birne, Blutwurz, Haselnuss, Himbeere, Mirabelle, Pflaume, Topinambur, Traube, Walnuss
Apple, pear, bloodroot, hazelnut, raspberry, mirabelle, plum, Jerusalem artichoke, grape, walnut

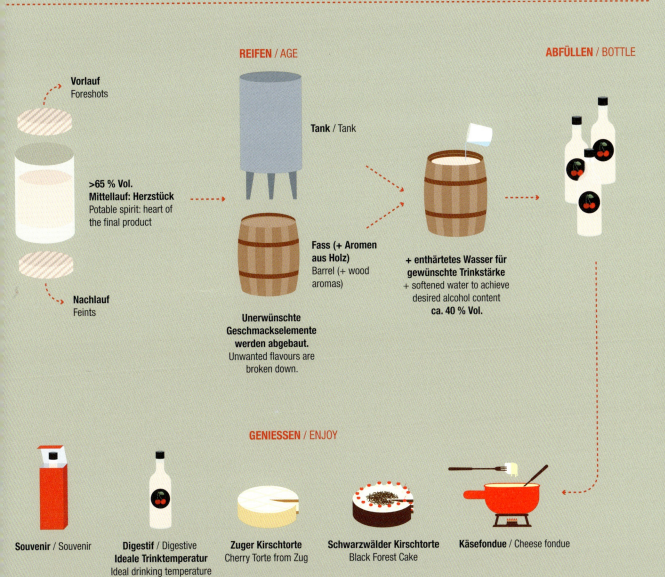

REIFEN / AGE
ABFÜLLEN / BOTTLE

Vorlauf / Foreshots

>65 % Vol. Mittellauf: Herzstück
Potable spirit: heart of the final product

Nachlauf / Feints

Tank / Tank

Fass (+ Aromen aus Holz)
Barrel (+ wood aromas)

Unerwünschte Geschmackselemente werden abgebaut.
Unwanted flavours are broken down.

+ enthärtetes Wasser für gewünschte Trinkstärke
+ softened water to achieve desired alcohol content
ca. 40 % Vol.

GENIESSEN / ENJOY

Souvenir / Souvenir

Digestif / Digestive
Ideale Trinktemperatur
Ideal drinking temperature
14–18° C

Zuger Kirschtorte
Cherry Torte from Zug

Schwarzwälder Kirschtorte
Black Forest Cake

Käsefondue / Cheese fondue

Kann ich bitte bestellen?
May I order please?

So is(s)t der Schwarzwald und sein Sternenhimmel.
The Black Forest is known for many specialities and a sky full of culinary stars.

2020
31
Michelin-Sterne
Michelin stars
26
Restaurants
Restaurants

- *Gasthof zum Storchen,* Bad Krozingen-Schmidhofen
- *Eckert,* Grenzach-Wyhlen
- *Restaurant Bareiss,* Baiersbronn-Mitteltal
- *Le Jardin de France,* Baden-Baden
- *Restaurant Sein,* Karlsruhe
- *Zehners Stube,* Pfaffenweiler
- *Der Öschberghof – Ösch Noir",* Donaueschingen
- *Alte Baiz,* Neuhausen-Hamberg
- *Genuss-Apotheke,* Bad Säckingen
- *Hotel Sackmann – Restaurant Schlossberg,* Baiersbronn-Schwarzenberg
- *Röttele's Restaurant & Residenz,* Baden-Baden
- *Ammolite Restaurant,* Rust
- *Gourmetrestaurant Berlins Krone,* Bad Teinach-Zavelstein

Schwarzwälder Tannenhonig
Kristallisiert nicht, enthält Mineralstoffe und Spuren von Harz
Black Forest fir honey
Doesn't crystallise, contains minerals and traces of resin

Bühler Zwetschgen
Buhl zwetschge plums

STRAUSSENWIRTSCHAFT
Bibbeleskäs
(Bibeliskäs, Bibbiliskäs, Bibeleskäs)
Alemannisch für Quark,
meist zubereitet mit Kräutern
und zu Brot gereicht
Alemannic for curd cheese,
usually mixed with herbs and
served with bread

GASTHAUS / INN
Elsässer Wurstsalat / Alsation sausage salad
Brägele / Fried potatoes
Schäufele / Traditional dish made from pork shoulder
Forelle / Trout
Saibling / Char

Traube Tonbach,
Schwarzwaldstube,
Baiersbronn*

Wolfshöhle,
Freiburg

Traube Tonbach,
Köhlerstube,
Baiersbronn*

Restaurant Erbprinz,
Ettlingen

Le Pavillon,
Bad Peterstal-Griesbach

Cedric Schwitzer's,
Waldbronn-Reichenbach

Merkles Restaurant,
Endingen

Hotel Restaurant Adler,
Lahr-Reichenbach

Traube Hotel & Restaurant,
Efringen-Kirchen

Restaurant Adler,
Häusern

* Wertung 2019,
Januar 2020 abgebrannt,
derzeit im „temporaire"
2019 rating, burned down
in January 2020,
temporary premises
called "temporaire"

Schloss Eberstein –
Werners Restaurant,
Gernsbach

Gasthaus
zum Raben,
Horben

Raubs Landgasthof,
Kuppenheim-Oberndorf

**
geschlossen,
Team kocht in
der Adler Stuben
closed, team
now cooking for
Adler Stuben

Parkhotel
Adler – Oscars,
Hinterzarten**

Restaurant Hirschen,
Sulzburg

BAUERNHOF / FARMYARD
Milch und Milchprodukte
Milk and dairy products

Best in the World –
Gourmand World
Cookbook Award

KOCHBÜCHER / COOKBOOKS
Schwarzwälder Tapas

Verena Scheidel und Manuel Wassmer kreieren Schwarzwälder Spezialitäten im Tapasformat.
Verena Scheidel and Manuel Wassmer
create Black Forest specialities
in the form of tapas.

Schwarzwälder Schinken
Black Forest Ham

Schwarzwälder Kirschtorte
Black Forest Cake

Einkehren beim Winzer
Stopping for a bite at the winery

In der Straußenwirtschaft (Strauße, Straußi, Besenwirtschaft, Kranzwirtschaft) gibt's regionale Köstlichkeiten. / Seasonal wine taverns known as "Straußenwirtschaft" serve regional specialities.

Der bunt geschmückte Reisigbesen zeigt an, dass geöffnet ist.
A colourfully decorated broom outside indicates that the tavern is open.

Speisen	Food
Flammkuchen	Tarte flambée
Bauernwurst	Farmhouse sausage
Schnitzel	Pork or veal cutlet
Spargel	Asparagus
Kartoffelsalat	Potato salad
Kässpätzle	Cheese spaetzle noodles
Spätzle mit Sauce	Spaetzle noodles with sauce
Bibbeleskäs	Curd cheese with herbs
Schäufele	Pork shoulder
Wurstsalat mit Brägele	Sausage salad with fried potatoes

Willkommen / Welcome

Glück im Spiel
The luck of the draw

Cego – das traditionelle Schwarzwälder Kartenspiel
Cego – the traditional Black Forest card game

TRÜMPFE / TRUMPS

Gstieß (Fool)

Farben und Trümpfe müssen bedient werden.
Suits and trumps must be played.

Kreuz / Clubs
König / King

Trock 1 / Mond (Moon)

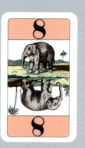

Kann Farbe nicht bedient werden, muss getrumpft werden.
If no card of the right suit can be played, then a trump must be played.

Dame / Queen

STECHEN / TRUMP

Kann weder bedient noch getrumpft werden, darf geschmiert werden.
If no suit or trump can be played, then a high-scoring card may be discarded.

Reiter / Knight

Geiß (Little Man)

Bube / Jack

TRÜMPFE STECHEN BILDERKARTEN UND LEERE / TRUMPS TRUMP FACE AND PIP CARDS.

Regeln können von Ort zu Ort variieren. Rules may vary from place to place.

 Spielrichtung Direction of play

 **oder** / or **Anzahl Spieler** Number of players

 **Schwarzwaldmeisterschaft** Black Forest Championship

 www.cego-online.de

BILDERKARTEN / FACE CARDS

Pik / Spades	**Herz** / Hearts	**Karo** / Diamonds

LEERE (KARTEN) / PIP CARDS

Kreuz / Clubs	**Pik** / Spades	**Herz** / Hearts	**Karo** / Diamonds

   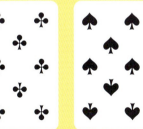   

STECHEN / TRUMP

BILDERKARTEN STECHEN LEERE / FACE CARDS TRUMP PIP CARDS.

Geschichte wird gemacht
History is made

Historische Ereignisse im Schwarzwald
Historic events in the Black Forest

Der Schwarzwald entsteht.
The Black Forest grows.

Alemannen und Franken
Alemanni and Franks

Freiburg erhält Stadtrecht.
Freiburg receives its town charter.

Wechselnde Zugehörigkeiten zu Frankreich, Vorderösterreich, Württemberg, Baden
Changing affiliations with France, Further Austria, Württemberg, Baden

| Vor 200–600 Mio. Jahren 200–600 million years ago | Bis 4. Jh. n. Chr. Until the 4th century AD | 4.–8. Jh. 4th – 8th century | 9. Jh. 9th century | 1218 | 1493–1517 | 16.–18. Jh. 16th – 18th century | 16. Jh. 16th century |

Kelten und Römer
Celts and Romans

Gründung des Klosters St. Trudpert im Münstertal
Founding of St. Trudpert's Abbey in Münstertal

Bundschuh-Bewegung
Bundschuh Movement

Herzogtum Württemberg wird protestantisch, Baden bleibt katholisch.
Duchy of Württemberg becomes Protestant, Baden remains Catholic.

| 726–1745 | 1818 | 1847 | 1848/49 | 1945 | 1950 | 1951 | 1952 | 1975 | 2002 |

Friedrich Hecker und Gustav Struve fordern in Offenburg die Selbstregierung des Volkes.
Friedrich Hecker and Gustav Struve in Offenburg advocate for self-government by the people.

Badische Revolution, Niederschlagung des Heckerzugs bei Kandern
Baden Revolution, defeat of the Hecker Uprising near Kandern

Gründung Baden-Württembergs
Founding of Baden-Württemberg

Beginn der Anti-Atomkraft-Bewegung: Erste Baustellen-Besetzung der Welt in Wyhl am Kaiserstuhl
Anti-nuclear movement launched: world's first occupied construction site, in Wyhl am Kaiserstuhl

Salpeterer-Aufstände
Saltpetre Wars

Bundesgerichtshof in Karlsruhe
Federal Court of Justice in Karlsruhe

Badische Verfassung in Karlsruhe
Baden Constitution in Karlsruhe

Volksabstimmung pro Südweststaat (Südbaden mehrheitlich contra)
The three states making up today's Baden-Württemberg vote in a referendum to merge (South Baden votes against).

Amerikanische und französische Besatzer teilen in drei Länder ein: Württemberg-Baden, (Süd-)Baden und Württemberg-Hohenzollern.
American and French occupiers divide the territory into three states: Württemberg-Baden, (South) Baden and Württemberg-Hohenzollern.

Bundesverfassungsgericht in Karlsruhe
Federal Constitutional Court in Karlsruhe

Erster Grüner Bürgermeister einer Großstadt: Freiburg
First Green Party mayor of a big city: Freiburg

Berühmte Schwarzwälder
Black Forest celebrities

Viele bleiben, manche gehen, andere werden heimisch.
Many stay, others leave, some end up making their home here.

BILDENDE KUNST
FINE ARTS

Hans Thoma
Franz Xaver Winterhalter
Hermann Dischler
Wilhelm Hasemann
Stefan Strumbel
Curt Liebich
Stephan Balkenhol
Katharina Grosse
Ulla von Brandenburg

POLITIK
POLITICS

Wolfgang Schäuble
Joseph Wirth
Constantin Fehrenbach
Ernst Benda
Gernot Erler
Joß Fritz

MUSIKER
MUSICIANS

Judith Holofernes
Dirk von Lowtzow
Walter Mossmann
Tony Marshall
Nino de Angelo
Laith Sascha Al-Deen
Max Giesinger
Max Mutzke
Anne-Sophie Mutter

BÜHNE & TV
STAGE & TV

Til Schweiger
Katharina Wackernagel
Johanna Wokalek
Nadeshda Brennicke
Sebastian Koch
Sasha Waltz
Ralf Bauer
Pierre Marcel Krause
Maren Ade
Jörg Kachelmann
Frank Elstner

FUßBALL
FOOTBALL

Oliver Kahn
Joshua Kimmich
Jogi Löw
Melanie Behringer
Christian Streich
Fritz Keller
Laura Anna Benkarth
Matthias Ginter
Dennis Aogo
Mehmet Scholl
Ottmar Hitzfeld
Jürgen Klopp

MODE
FASHION

Kim Schimpfle
Aenne Burda
Jochen Scherzinger
Sandy Dietrich
Anna Ewers

LITERATUR
LITERATURE

Hermann Hesse
Benjamin Lebert
Silke Scheuermann
Marie Luise Kaschnitz
Rüdiger Safranski
Peter Sloterdijk
Martin Heidegger
Johann Peter Hebel
Joseph Victor von Scheffel
Swetlana Geier
Heinrich Hansjakob

WINTERSPORT
WINTER SPORTS

Georg Thoma
Dieter Thoma
Simone Hauswald
Martin Schmitt
Fabian Rießle
Stefanie Böhler
Marcel, Sascha & Nikolai Goc
Benedikt Doll
Sandra Ringwald
Georg Hettich

SOMMERSPORT
SUMMER SPORTS

Sabine Spitz
Regina Halmich
Eva Rösken
Steffen Fetzner
Martin Schwab
Benjamin Rudiger
Julian Schelb
Adelheid Morath
Simon Stiebjahn

Der Weltmeister ist ein Waldmeister

The world champion is a Black Forest native

Joachim „Jogi" Löw hat schon auf der ganzen Welt gearbeitet, ist seiner Heimat aber treu geblieben. Er lebt in Freiburg.
Joachim "Jogi" Löw has worked all over the world but has remained true to his home region. He lives in Freiburg.

3.2.1960
Geboren in Schönau im Schwarzwald
Born in Schönau in the Black Forest

STATIONEN ALS FUßBALLPROFI
STATIONS AS A PRO FOOTBALL PLAYER

SC Freiburg
1978–80
1982–84
1985–89

VfB Stuttgart
1980–81

Eintracht Frankfurt
1981–82

Karlsruher SC
1984–85

FC Schaffhausen
1989–1992

FC Winterthur
1992–1994

STATIONEN ALS FUßBALLTRAINER
STATIONS AS A FOOTBALL COACH

1994
Spielertrainer beim FC Frauenfeld/CH
Player-coach for FC Frauenfeld/CH

1997
DFB-Pokal-Sieger mit VfB Stuttgart
DFB-Pokal winner with VfB Stuttgart

1998
Finalist im Europapokal der Pokalsieger
Finalist im UEFA Cup Winners' Cup
(Chelsea FC–VfB Stuttgart 1:0)

Trainer bei Fenerbahçe Istanbul und einer von nur zwei Trainern, die in dieser Saison nicht vorzeitig entlassen wurden
Manager of Fenerbahçe Istanbul and one of only two coaches not dismissed early in the season

1999
Vorzeitige Entlassung beim Karlsruher SC (2. Bundesliga) nach nur 1 Sieg in 18 Spielen
Early dismissal as manager of Karlsruher SC (2nd Bundesliga) after only 1 win in 18 matches

2002
Österreichischer Meister mit FC Tirol Innsbruck, der kurz darauf Konkurs anmeldet
Austrian champion with FC Tirol Innsbruck, which shortly thereafter declared bankruptcy

2014 **
Weltmeister in Brasilien
World champion in Brazil
(Deutschland–Argentinien 1:0)

Fußballtrainer und FIFA-Trainer des Jahres
FIFA World Coach of the Year

2012
EM in Polen/Ukraine, im Halbfinale ausgeschieden
Euro 2012 in Poland/Ukraine, eliminated in the semi-finals
(Deutschland–Italien 1:2)

2016
EM in Frankreich, im Halbfinale ausgeschieden
Euro 2016 in France, eliminated in the semi-finals
(Deutschland–Frankreich 0:2)

2010
3. Platz bei der WM in Südafrika
3rd place in the World Cup in South Africa
(Uruguay–Deutschland 2:3)

2017 **
Confed-Cup-Sieger
Confederations Cup winner
(Chile–Deutschland 0:1)

2008
2. Platz bei der EM als Cheftrainer der deutschen Nationalmannschaft
Runner-up in Euro 2008 as head manager of the German national team
(Deutschland–Spanien 0:1)

2018
WM in Russland: in der Gruppenphase ausgeschieden
World Cup in Russia: eliminated in the group stage

2006
3. Platz bei der WM als Co-Trainer der deutschen Nationalmannschaft
3rd place in the World Cup as assistant manager of the German national team
(Deutschland–Portugal 3:1)

2020
Dienstältester Nationaltrainer der Welt
Longest-serving national team coach in the world

**
Welt-Nationaltrainer
World Cup national team coach

2005
3. Platz beim Confed Cup als Co-Trainer der deutschen Nationalmannschaft
3rd place in the Confederations Cup as assistant manager of the German national team

2003–2004
Austria Wien
Manager of Austria Wien

Jogi-Löw-Stadion

So heißt das Stadion des FC Schönau 08 seit 2014.
Name of the FC Schönau 08 stadium since 2014

11 Freunde sollt ihr sein
You have to be 11 friends

Der Sport-Club Freiburg ist einer der sympathischsten Vereine Deutschlands. / Sport-Club Freiburg is one of Germany's most likeable football clubs.

Stadion / Stadium

Der SC Freiburg spielte lange Zeit im Schwarzwald-Stadion. 2021 Umzug ins neue Stadion (34.700 Plätze).
SC Freiburg has played in the Black Forest Stadium for many years. The club is set to move to a new stadium in 2021.

Allstar-Elf / All-star Team

Nils Petersen
Jogi Löw

Rodolfo Esteban Cardoso
Zoubaier Baya
Levan Kobiashvili
Jens Todt

Nicolas Höfler
Andreas Zeyer
Boubacar Diarra
Charly Schulz

Richard Golz

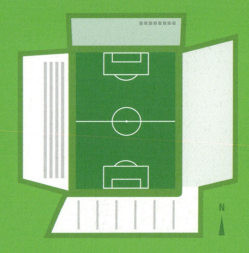

Aufs und Abs / Ups and downs
(Zusatzinfos beziehen sich nur auf Herrenmannschaft / The additional information refers to the men's team only)

Längste Trainer / Longest-serving coaches
Volker Finke (16 Jahre / years), so lange wie kein anderer in Deutschland / longest term of service of any trainer in Germany
1.7.1991–30.6.2007

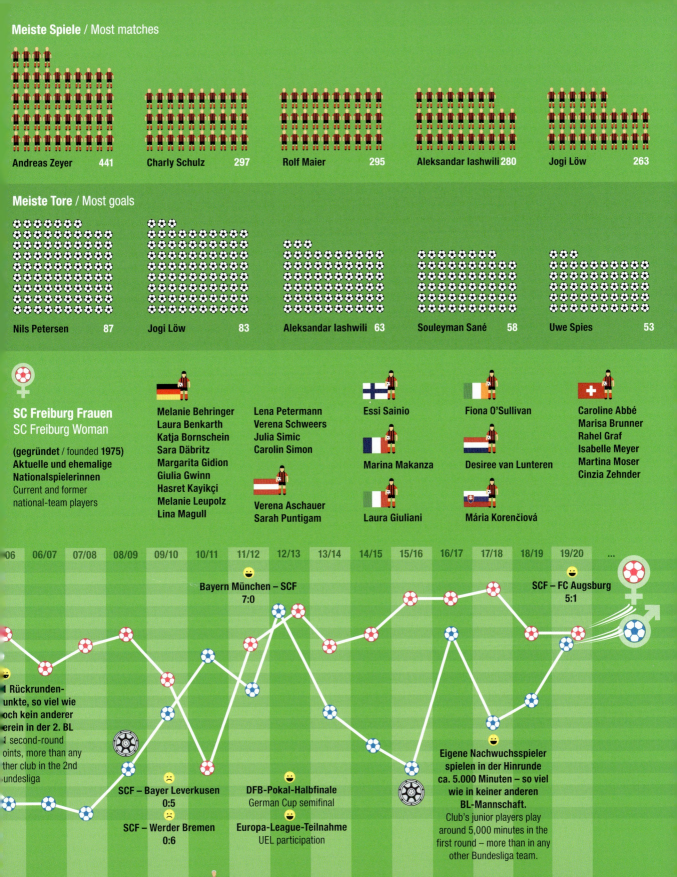

Die Wiege des Skisports
The cradle of skiing

Im Schwarzwald wurde das Skifahren erfunden. / The Black Forest is the cradle of the sport of skiing.

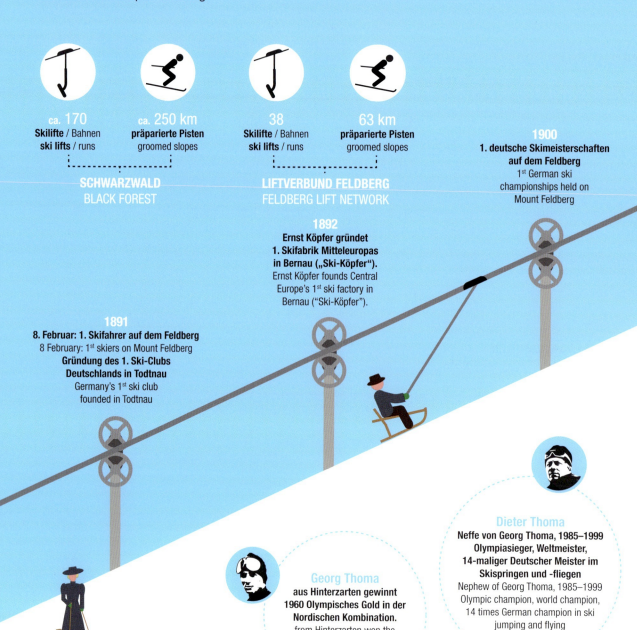

ca. 170
Skilifte / Bahnen
ski lifts / runs

ca. 250 km
präparierte Pisten
groomed slopes

SCHWARZWALD
BLACK FOREST

38
Skilifte / Bahnen
ski lifts / runs

63 km
präparierte Pisten
groomed slopes

LIFTVERBUND FELDBERG
FELDBERG LIFT NETWORK

1900
1. deutsche Skimeisterschaften auf dem Feldberg
1st German ski championships held on Mount Feldberg

1892
Ernst Köpfer gründet 1. Skifabrik Mitteleuropas in Bernau („Ski-Köpfer").
Ernst Köpfer founds Central Europe's 1st ski factory in Bernau ("Ski-Köpfer").

1891
8. Februar: 1. Skifahrer auf dem Feldberg
8 February: 1st skiers on Mount Feldberg
Gründung des 1. Ski-Clubs Deutschlands in Todtnau
Germany's 1st ski club founded in Todtnau

Georg Thoma
aus Hinterzarten gewinnt 1960 Olympisches Gold in der Nordischen Kombination.
from Hinterzarten won the Olympic gold medal in the Nordic combined in 1960.

Dieter Thoma
Neffe von Georg Thoma, 1985–1999 Olympiasieger, Weltmeister, 14-maliger Deutscher Meister im Skispringen und -fliegen
Nephew of Georg Thoma, 1985–1999 Olympic champion, world champion, 14 times German champion in ski jumping and flying

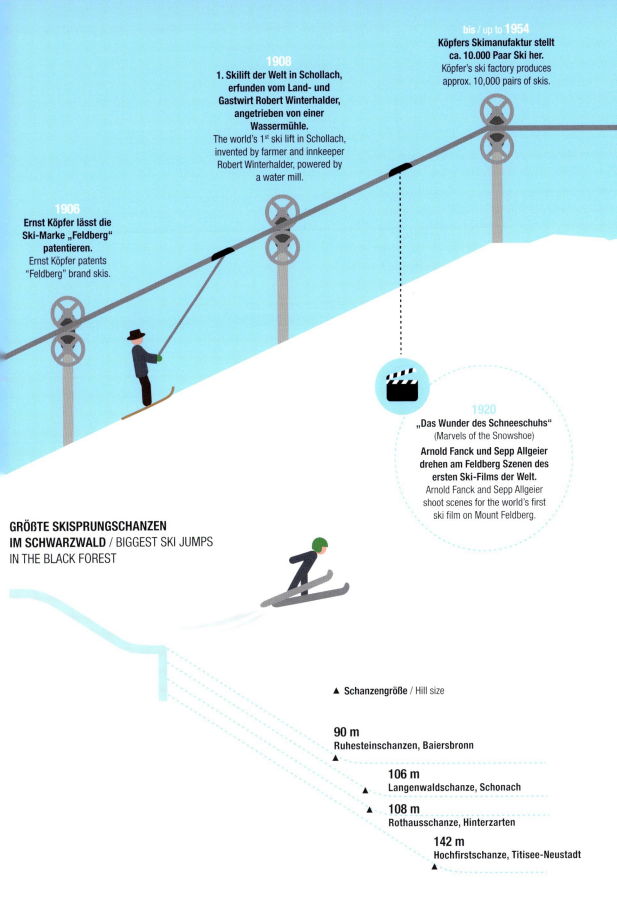

Alle reden vom Wetter
Everyone's talking about the weather

So unterschiedlich ist das Klima in der Ferienregion Schwarzwald.
The Black Forest holiday region has a surprisingly wide range of climates.

NATIONALPARK UND FELDBERG
NATIONAL PARK AND FELDBERG
Im Herbst und Winter häufig Inversionswetterlage
Frequent inversions in autumn and winter

Obere Luftschichten wärmer …
Upper layers of air warmer …

… untere kühler
… lower layers cooler

Nebel / Fog

Das Klima des Schwarzwalds ist ozeanisch geprägt: hohe Niederschlagsmengen und relativ milde Winter.
The Black Forest in general has an oceanic climate with high rainfall and relatively mild winters.

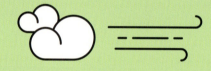

Frankreich / France

Vogesen / Vosges

Legende / Legend

 Jahresdurchschnittstemperatur
Average annual temperature

 Durchschnittlicher Jahresniederschlag
Average annual precipitation

 Regentage
Average days of rain/year

 Durchschnittliche Sonnenscheindauer/Jahr
Average sunshine hours/year

 Durchschnittliche Sonnenscheindauer/Tag
Average sunshine hours/day

 Atlantische Westwinde mit feuchten Luftmassen
Atlantic west winds bring humid air masses

 Wolken regnen ab.
Clouds releasing rain

 Wenig Niederschlag
Little precipitation

 Hagelabwehr / Hail suppression squad
Fliegt in Gewitterwolken und versprüht eine Silberjodid-Verbindung → verhindert Bildung großer Hagelkörner.
Flies into thunderclouds to seed them with silver iodide particles → preventing the formation of large hailstones

FREIBURG
 11,6° C
 900 mm
Eine der wärmsten Städte Deutschlands
One of the warmest towns in Germany

FELDBERG
 3,9° C
 2.000 mm
 Max.: 27,4° C
(Juli / July 1983)
 Tiefste / Lowest:
−30,7° C
(Februar / February 1956)

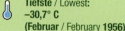

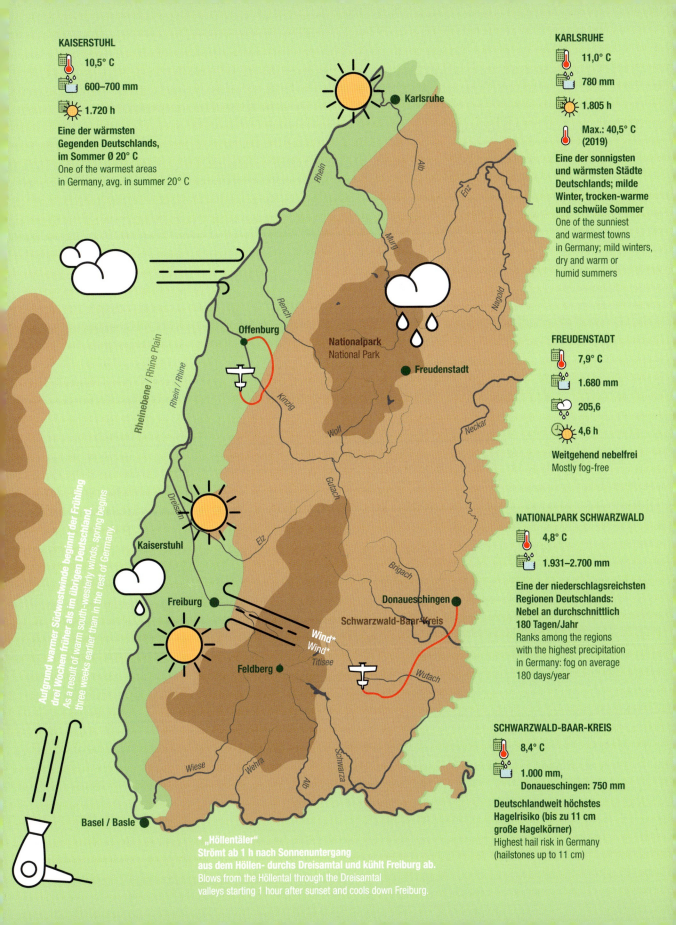

Nichts liegt näher als der Bahnhof
The next train station is just around the corner

Mancherorts erinnert der Schwarzwald an eine Miniatureisenbahnlandschaft. / In some spots the Black Forest resembles a model railroad landscape.

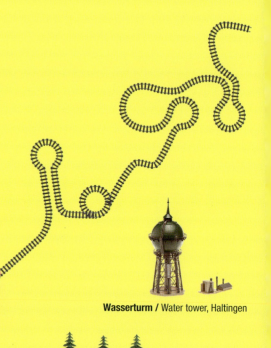

61,7 km — **Wutachtalbahn (Sauschwänzlebahn)** Wutach Valley Railway (lit. Pigtail Line): **Waldshut-Tiengen–Immendingen**

Wasserturm / Water tower, Haltingen

186,4 km

149 km

19,76 km — **Enztalbahn** / Enz Valley Railway: **Pforzheim–Bad Wildbad**

25,8 km — **Albtalbahn** / Alb Valley Railway: **Karlsruhe–Bad Herrenalb**

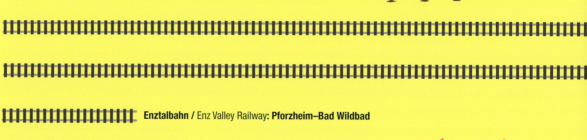

58 km — **Murgtalbahn** / Murg Valley Railway: **Rastatt–Freudenstadt**

10,7 km — **Achertalbahn** / Acher Valley Railway: **Achern–Ottenhöfen**

29,1 km — **Renchtalbahn** / Rench Valley Railway: **Appenweier–Bad Griesbach**

39,1 km — **Kinzigtalbahn** / Kinzig Valley Railway: **Hausach–Freudenstadt**

19,3 km — **Elztalbahn** / Elz Valley Railway: **Denzlingen–Elzach**

Höllentalbahn / lit.: Hell Valley Railway: **Freiburg–Donaueschingen**
76,2 km

5,8 km — **Münstertalbahn** / Münstertal Railway: **Bad Krozingen–Münstertal**

1946

gründen die Gebrüder Faller aus Gütenbach eine Firma, die Häuser für Modelleisenbahnlandschaften herstellt. Viele davon haben reale Gebäude des Schwarzwalds zum Vorbild.
The Faller Brothers from Gütenbach establish a company that makes miniature buildings for model railroads. Many are based on real buildings in the Black Forest.

1.200.000
Häuser pro Jahr
buildings per year

Martinstor / St. Martin's gate, Freiburg

Kino / cinema Kandelhof, Freiburg

Öhlermühle / Öhler Mill, Jostal

100
Mitarbeiter
employees

Hexenlochmühle / Hexenloch Mill

Schwarzwaldhof mit Strohdach / Black Forest farm with straw roof

1. Weltgrößte Kuckucksuhr / 1st Biggest cuckoo clock in the world, Schonach

Rheintalstrecke / Rhine Valley Railway: **Karlsruhe–Basel**

Badische Schwarzwaldbahn / Baden Black Forest Railway: **Offenburg–Konstanz**

56,66 km **Nagoldtalbahn** / Nagold Valley Railway: **Pforzheim–Horb**

12,9 km **Kandertalbahn** / Kander Valley Railway: **Haltingen–Kandern** (Private Museumseisenbahn / private heritage railway)

28,75 km **Wiesentalbahn** / Wiese Valley Railway: **Basel–Zell im Wiesental**

19,2 km **Dreiseenbahn** / Three Lakes Railway: **Titisee–Seebrugg**

26,78 km **Bahnstrecke** / Railway: **Rottweil–Villingen**

29,9 km **Gäubahn (Zweigstrecke)** / Gäu Railway (branch line): **Eutingen–Freudenstadt**

ca. 45 km **Streckenabschnitt der Gäubahn** / Track section of the Gäu Railway Stuttgart–Tuttlingen: **Horb am Neckar–Rottweil**

10,6 km **Harmersbachtalbahn** / Harmersbach Valley Railway: **Biberach (Baden)–Oberharmersbach-Riersbach**

ca. 20 km **Hermann-Hesse-Bahn** / Hermann Hesse Railway: **Weil der Stadt–Calw** (ab / from 2023)

Kreuz und quer
Traversing the region

Ferienstraßen im Schwarzwald / Holiday routes in the Black Forest

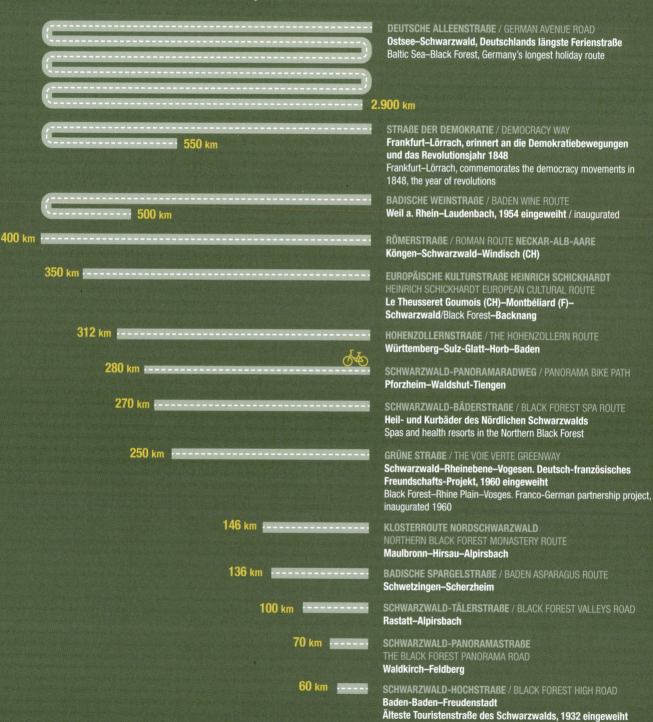

DEUTSCHE ALLEENSTRAßE / GERMAN AVENUE ROAD
Ostsee–Schwarzwald, Deutschlands längste Ferienstraße
Baltic Sea–Black Forest, Germany's longest holiday route
2.900 km

550 km
STRAßE DER DEMOKRATIE / DEMOCRACY WAY
Frankfurt–Lörrach, erinnert an die Demokratiebewegungen und das Revolutionsjahr 1848
Frankfurt–Lörrach, commemorates the democracy movements in 1848, the year of revolutions

500 km
BADISCHE WEINSTRAßE / BADEN WINE ROUTE
Weil a. Rhein–Laudenbach, 1954 eingeweiht / inaugurated

400 km
RÖMERSTRAßE / ROMAN ROUTE NECKAR-ALB-AARE
Köngen–Schwarzwald–Windisch (CH)

350 km
EUROPÄISCHE KULTURSTRAßE HEINRICH SCHICKHARDT
HEINRICH SCHICKHARDT EUROPEAN CULTURAL ROUTE
Le Theusseret Goumois (CH)–Montbéliard (F)–Schwarzwald/Black Forest–Backnang

312 km
HOHENZOLLERNSTRAßE / THE HOHENZOLLERN ROUTE
Württemberg–Sulz-Glatt–Horb–Baden

280 km
SCHWARZWALD-PANORAMARADWEG / PANORAMA BIKE PATH
Pforzheim–Waldshut-Tiengen

270 km
SCHWARZWALD-BÄDERSTRAßE / BLACK FOREST SPA ROUTE
Heil- und Kurbäder des Nördlichen Schwarzwalds
Spas and health resorts in the Northern Black Forest

250 km
GRÜNE STRAßE / THE VOIE VERTE GREENWAY
Schwarzwald–Rheinebene–Vogesen. Deutsch-französisches Freundschafts-Projekt, 1960 eingeweiht
Black Forest–Rhine Plain–Vosges. Franco-German partnership project, inaugurated 1960

146 km
KLOSTERROUTE NORDSCHWARZWALD
NORTHERN BLACK FOREST MONASTERY ROUTE
Maulbronn–Hirsau–Alpirsbach

136 km
BADISCHE SPARGELSTRAßE / BADEN ASPARAGUS ROUTE
Schwetzingen–Scherzheim

100 km
SCHWARZWALD-TÄLERSTRAßE / BLACK FOREST VALLEYS ROAD
Rastatt–Alpirsbach

70 km
SCHWARZWALD-PANORAMASTRAßE
THE BLACK FOREST PANORAMA ROAD
Waldkirch–Feldberg

60 km
SCHWARZWALD-HOCHSTRAßE / BLACK FOREST HIGH ROAD
Baden-Baden–Freudenstadt
Älteste Touristenstraße des Schwarzwalds, 1932 eingeweiht
Oldest tourist route in the Black Forest, inaugurated in 1932

Villingen-Schwenningen
Uhrenindustriemuseum
Museum of Clockmaking

Deißlingen
Uhrenkundliches Museum
Clock Museum

Trossingen
Harmonika-Museum
und Schwarzwälder
Uhren-Sammlung
Harmonica Museum
and Black Forest
Clock Collection

Vöhrenbach
Uhrmacherhäusle von 1726
Clockmaker's house from 1726

Unterkirnach
Orchestrionmuseum
Orchestrion Museum

Eisenbach
Weltzeituhr von 1865
World clock from 1865

Rottweil
Stadtarchiv mit Sonnenuhr
Town archive with sundial

Titisee-Neustadt
Heimatstube mit
Uhrmacherwerkstatt
Country parlour with
clockmakers' workshop

Niedereschach
Rathaus mit Kirchturmuhrwerk
Town hall with church clock

Lenzkirch
Uhrenfreunde Lenzkirch
Lenzkirch Clock
Enthusiasts Club

Königsfeld
Dorfmuseum mit Uhren
aus zwei Jahrhunderten
Village museum with clocks
spanning two centuries

St. Märgen
Klostermuseum mit
Uhrensammlung
Monastery Museum
with clock collection

St. Georgen
Deutsches Phonomuseum
German Phono Museum

St. Peter
Orgeluhr
Organ clock

Schramberg
Uhrenfabrik, Uhrenwelt,
Uhrenmuseum
& Uhrengeschichte
Clock factory, clock world,
Clock Museum & history
of clockmaking

2 8 5 km
DEUTSCHE UHRENSTRASSE
GERMAN CLOCK ROAD

Waldkirch
Drehorgel und
Musikautomaten
Barrel organ and
mechanical instruments

Lauterbach
Ehemaliges Rathaus
mit Standuhr
Former town hall
with grandfather clock

Simonswald
Uhrmacherwerkstatt
Clockmakers'
workshop

Hornberg
Uhrenspiele
Giant cuckoo clock

Gütenbach
Dorfmuseum mit
Kuckucksuhren
und Spieluhren
Village museum
with cuckoo clocks
and music boxes

Triberg
Schwarzwaldmuseum
mit Lack-, Spiel- und
Kuckucksuhren
Black Forest Museum
with lacquer, musical
and cuckoo clocks

Schönwald
Hier wurde 1737
die Kuckucksuhr
erfunden.
The cuckoo clock
was invented here
in 1737.

Schonach
Weltgrößte Kuckucksuhr
World's largest cuckoo clock

Furtwangen
Deutsches
Uhrenmuseum
The German
Clock Museum

Wegweisend
Trailblazing

Der Schwarzwaldverein ist der älteste Wanderverein Deutschlands. / The Black Forest Hiking Club is the oldest of its kind in Germany.

1864
Gründung Badischer Schwarzwaldverein in Freiburg
Founding of the Baden Black Forest Hiking Club in Freiburg

1884
Gründung Württembergischer Schwarzwaldverein in Stuttgart
Founding of the Württemberg Black Forest Hiking Club in Stuttgart

1934
Zusammenschluss zu Schwarzwaldverein e.V.
Merger to form the Black Forest Hiking Club e.V.

AKTIVITÄTEN / ACTIVITIES

26 Wanderheime mit ca 30.000 Übernachtungen pro Jahr
Cabins with around 30,000 overnight stays/year

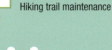
Wanderweg-Betreuung
Hiking trail maintenance

Familien- und Jugendarbeit
Family and youth work

Heimatpflege
Fostering local heritage

Wanderkarten
Hiking maps

Wanderungen
Hikes

Vereinszeitschrift „Der Schwarzwald", erscheint vierteljährlich
Club magazine "Der Schwarzwald" published quarterly

Naturschutz
Nature conservation

STRUKTUR / STRUCTURE

ca. 210 Ortsvereine
local clubs

ca. 60.000 Mitglieder
members

BETREUTE WANDERWEGE / SUPERVISED HIKING TRAILS

24.000 km im Schwarzwald und in angrenzenden Landschaften
in the Black Forest and adjacent regions

15.500 Wegweiserstandorte
signposts

30.000 ehrenamtlich geleistete Arbeitsstunden
volunteer hours worked

Alle mit einer Raute markiert
All marked with a diamond

Örtliche Wanderwege
Local hiking trails

Regionale Wanderwege
Regional hiking trails

Fernwanderwege
Long-distance hiking trails

Eigentümer
Owners
Feldberggipfel
Feldberg summit

EINIGE PROTESTE UND AKTIONEN
A FEW PROTESTS AND CAMPAIGNS

1912 — Protest gegen den Bau des Murgtalkraftwerks
Protest against the construction of the Murgtal Power Plant

 Einspruch gegen Staustufen im Monbachtal
Appeal against barrages in the Monbach Valley — **1927**

1954 — Verhinderung eines Sessellifts am Belchen
Prevention of a chair lift to the Belchen summit

 Sperrung von Waldwegen für Kfz
Forest roads closed to motor vehicles

 Bemühungen um die Schaffung eines Naturparks „Nordschwarzwald"
Efforts to create a Northern Black Forest nature reserve — **1972**

1973 — Widerstand gegen eine Schwarzwaldautobahn (Freiburg–Donaueschingen), 1983 abgelehnt
Resistance against a Black Forest motorway (Freiburg-Donaueschingen), rejected in 1983

 Kundgebung zum Waldsterben auf dem Thurner unter Beteiligung von Bundespräsident Richard von Weizsäcker
Demonstration against forest dieback on the Thurner Pass, joined by German President Richard von Weizsäcker — **1986**

2009 — Resolution zur „Erhaltung der offenen Landschaft im Schwarzwald"
Resolution on the "Preservation of open landscape in the Black Forest"

 Kongress zur Energiewende, u. a. Positionierung zum Ausbau der Windkraft
Conference on the energy revolution, incl. positioning on expansion of wind power — **2011**

2013 — Flankierende Maßnahmen zur Einrichtung des Nationalparks Schwarzwald
Measures flanking the establishment of the Black Forest National Park

 Kritische Position zur Rückkehr des Wolfes in den Schwarzwald
Critical position on the return of the wolf to the Black Forest — **2019**

Der Weg ist das Ziel
The journey is the reward

Der Schwarzwald ist eine der vielseitigsten Wanderregionen Deutschlands. / The Black Forest offers hikers more variety than almost anywhere else in Germany.

285 km Westweg — 1900 angelegt / created
Pforzheim→Dobel→Forbach→Unterstmatt→Alexanderschanze→Hausach→Wilhelmshöhe→Kalte Herberge→→Hinterzarten→Wiedener Eck→Kandern→→Bärental→Weißenbachsattel→Hasel↗ **Basel**

245 km Ostweg
Pforzheim→Bad Liebenzell→Oberhaugstett→Pfalzgrafenweiler→Freudenstadt→Alpirsbach→Schramberg→Villingen-Schwenningen→→Bad Dürrheim→Geisingen→Achdorf-Stühlingen→**Schaffhausen**

233 km Mittelweg
Pforzheim→Bad Wildbad→Besenfeld→Zwieselberg→Schiltach→St. Georgen→Kalte Herberge→Lenzkirch→↗Häusern↘→Grafenhausen→**Waldshut**

180 km Querweg Freiburg–Bodensee
Freiburg→Hinterzarten→Wutachschlucht→Blumberg→Engen→Singen→Langenrain→**Konstanz**

160 km Rheinauenweg
Kehl→Ichenheim→Kappel-Grafenhausen→Wyhl→Breisach→Grißheim→→Bad Bellingen→**Weil am Rhein**

125 km Hochrhein-Höhenweg
Basel→Rheinfelden→Rickenbach→Dogern→Bechtersbohl→→Lottstetten→**Schaffhausen**

120 km Gäurandweg
Mühlacker→Tiefenbronn→Stammheim→Nagold→→Waldachtal→**Freudenstadt**

118 km Schluchtensteig
Stühlingen→Blumberg→Schattenmühle→Schluchsee→St. Blasien→→Todtmoos→**Wehr**

110 km Kandelhöhenweg
Freiburg→St. Peter→Waldkirch→Höhehäuser→→Gengenbach→**Oberkirch**

110 km Murgleiter
Gaggenau→Gernsbach→Forbach→Schönmünzach→→Baiersbronn→**Schliffkopf**

109 km Querweg Schwarzwald–Kaiserstuhl–Rhein
Donaueschingen→Vöhrenbach→Simonswald→Denzlingen→→Oberrottweil→**Breisach**

108 km WasserWeltenSteig
Triberg→Brend→Hammereisenbach→Unterbränd→Achdorf→→Siblinger Randenhaus→**Neuhausen am Rheinfall**

108 km Zweitälersteig
Waldkirch→Kandel→Simonswald→Oberprechtal-Wittenbach→→Höhenhäuser→**Waldkirch**

99 km Breisgauer Weinweg
Freiburg→Vöhrenbach→Mundingen→Nordweil→→Ettenheim→Lahr→**Diersburg**

99 km Ortenauer Weinpfad
Gernsbach→Baden-Baden→Neusatz→Oberkirch→→Zell-Weierbach→Gengenbach→**Diersburg**

98 km Renchtalsteig
Oberkirch→Oppenau→Bad Peterstal→Alexanderschanze→→Allerheiligen-Wasserfälle→**Burgruine Schauenberg**

96 km Großer Hans-Jakob-Weg
Haslach→Brandenkopf→Zell a.H.→Höhenhäuser→**Haslach**

94 km Querweg Lahr–Rottweil
Lahr→Höhenhäuser→Hornberg→Buchenberg→**Rottweil**

92 km Markgräfler Wii-Wegli
Freiburg→Staufen→Müllheim→Bad Bellingen→→Ötlingen→**Grenzach-Wyhlen**

91 km Baiersbronner Seensteig
Baiersbronn→Mitteltal→Schliffkopf→Mummelsee→→Schönmünzach→**Baiersbronn**

83 km Albsteig Schwarzwald
Albbruck→Görwihl→Wittenschwand→→St. Blasien→Bernau→**Feldberg**

56 km Schwarzwald-Nordrandweg
Mühlacker→Pforzheim→→Langensteinbach→**Durlach**

52 km Kleiner Hans-Jakob-Weg
Schapbach→Schenkenzell→→St. Roman→**Schapbach**

23 km Schneckenwanderweg *
Schönwald→Triberger Wasserfälle→Blindensee→Elzquelle→→Bregquelle→Martinskapelle→**Schönwald**

* der langsamste Wanderweg des Schwarzwalds / slowest hiking trail in the Black Forest

Der Schwarzwald von oben
The Black Forest from above

Türme, Plattformen und Terrassen mit sagenhaften Ausblicken (Auswahl)
Towers, platforms and terraces offering fabulous views (a selection)

Nordschwarzwald / Northern Black Forest, **Rheinebene** / Rhine Plain, **Vogesen** / Vosges, **Mehliskopf, Hornisgrinde, Großer Feldberg (Taunus), Pfälzerwald** / Palatinate Forest, **Schwäbische Alb** / Swabian Jura, **Schweizer Alpen** / Swiss Alps

Friedrichsturm
Frederick's Tower
Baden-Baden
30 m

29 m / 168

Vitra Design Museum

Vitra Rutschturm
Vitra Slide Tower
Weil am Rhein
31 m

17 m / 85

Feldberg, Freiburg, Vogesen / Vosges, **Kaiserstuhl, Münstertal** / Münster Valley

Eugen-Keidel-Turm
Eugen Keidel Tower
Schauinsland
31 m

22 m / 85

Rheinebene / Rhine Plain, **Kandel, Vogesen** / Vosges

Urenkopfturm
Urenkopf Tower
Haslach
34,5 m

33 m / 183

Freiburg: Münster, Wiehre; Kaiserstuhl, Vogesen / Vosges, **Rheinebene** / Rhine Plain

Schlossbergturm
Castle Hill Tower
Freiburg
35 m

35 m / 153

Schwarzwald-Rundumblick
A panoramic view of the Black Forest

Baumwipfelpfad-Aussichtsturm
Treetop walk observation tower
Bad Wildbad
38 m

37 m / 0

Kaiserstuhl, Breisgauer Bucht, Wald / forest, **Vogesen** / Vosges, **Straßburger Münster** / Strasbourg Cathedral, **Hornisgrinde, Schweizer Jura** / Jura Mountains

Eichelspitzturm
Eichstetten
42,5 m

28 m / 127

Feldberg, Rheintal / Rhine Valley, **Schweizer Alpen** / Swiss Alps, **Mont Blanc, Säntis, Kletterer an der Turmwand** / climbers clinging to the tower

Rothaus-Zäpfle-Turm
Rothaus
51 m

42 m / 249

Breisgauer Bucht, Kandel, Schweizer Jura / Jura Mountains, **Vogesen** / Vosges, **Kaiserstuhl**

Höchster reiner Aussichtsturm Deutschlands
Germany's tallest dedicated observation tower

Eichbergturm
Emmendingen
53,2 m

43,2 m / 240

Titisee, Schluchsee, Österreichische Alpen / Austrian Alps, **Berner Oberland** / Bernese Oberland, **Mont-Blanc-Massiv** / Mont Blanc massif, **Vogesen** / Vosges

mit Trauzimmer
with wedding room

Feldbergturm
Feldberg
50 m

45 m / 175

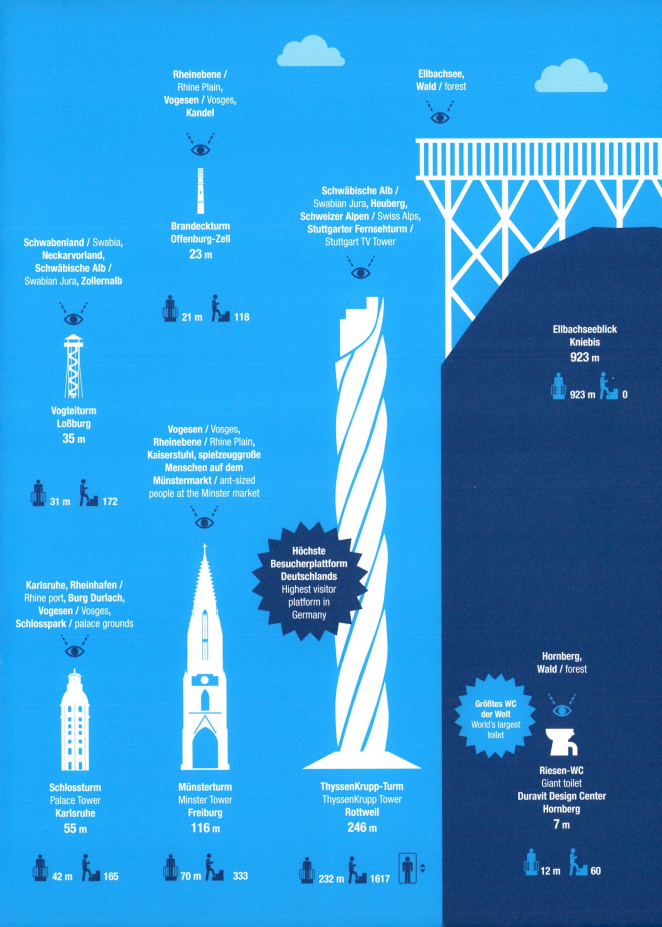

Ein schöner Zeitvertreib
A good time for all

Im Europa-Park und in der Wasserwelt Rulantica in Rust dreht sich alles um die Freizeit. / At Europa-Park and Waterworld Rulantica in Rust it's all about fun, fun, fun.

Eröffnet am 12. Juli 1975 von Franz Mack
Opened on 12 July 1975 by Franz Mack

Besucherstärkster saisonaler Freizeitpark der Welt
Most popular seasonal theme park in the world

Gemeinde Rust bei Freiburg, an der Autobahn A5, im Dreiländereck Deutschland-Frankreich-Schweiz
Town of Rust near Freiburg, on the A5 motorway, where the borders of Germany, France and Switzerland meet

> 5.700.000
Besucherzahl 2019
visitors in 2019

> 115.000.000
Besucher seit Eröffnung
visitors since opening

140 ha
Gesamtfläche
total area

Nationalität der Besucher 2019
Visitor nationalities 2019

50 %	
Deutschland Germany	
22 %	
Frankreich France	
22 %	
Schweiz Switzerland	
6 %	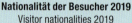
Sonstige Other	

29 Jahre / years
Altersdurchschnitt der Besucher
average age of visitors

4.450
Mitarbeiter in der Saison
employees each season

Einer der 25 besucherstärksten Freizeitparks der Welt
One of the 25 most popular theme parks in the world

8,5 Stunden / hours
durchschnittliche Aufenthaltsdauer
average length of stay

2,2 Stunden / hours
durchschnittliche Anreisedauer
average travel time

ATTRAKTIONEN / ATTRACTIONS

Meistbesuchter Freizeitpark im deutschsprachigen Raum
Most popular theme park in the German-speaking countries

> 100 Attraktionen & Shows / Attractions & shows
23 Stunden Showprogramm täglich / hours of shows daily
1 Kino / cinema

Zweitbesucherstärkster Freizeitpark Europas
Europe's second most popular theme park

 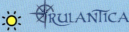

Die Wasserwelt / The Waterworld — RULANTICA — **17** Wasserrutschen / water slides

1 Außenbecken (500 m²) / outdoor pool (500 m²)
1 Wellenbad / wave pool

1 Strömungskanal / flow channel

Rust hat den bundesweit ersten deutsch-französischen Polizeiposten: Im Sommer 8 deutsche Polizisten und mindestens 2 Gendarmen aus Frankreich.
Rust has the first Franco-German police station in Germany, with 8 German police officers and at least 2 gendarmes from France in the summer.

DER SCHWARZWALD IM EUROPA-PARK / THE BLACK FOREST AT EUROPAPARK

MADE IN SCHWARZWALD / MADE IN THE BLACK FOREST

Jährlicher Verbrauch / Annual consumption

 141.058 l Milch / milk
 6 t Speck / bacon
 926 Kirschtorten / Black Forest Cake
 120 kg Honig / honey
 11 t Marmelade/Konfitüre / jam
 240 l Schnaps / liquor
 2.821 kg Schinken / ham
 2.157 kg Schäufele / pork shoulder

GASTRONOMIE / GASTRONOMY

 6 Hotels / hotels
 4 Restaurants / restaurants
  davon Sterne-Restaurants / thereof gourmet restaurants **1**
 10 Selbstbedienungs-restaurants / self-service restaurants
 ≈ 5.800 Gästebetten / guest beds
 7 Cafés & Bars / cafés & bars
 26 Imbisse / snack bars
 9 Eisdielen / ice cream parlours
 7 Verkaufsstände / food stands

2014–2019 „Golden Ticket Award"
Bester Freizeitpark weltweit
Best Amusement Park in the world

Narri, Narro!

Die schwäbisch-alemannische Fasnacht
The Swabian-Alemannic Carnival

GESCHICHTE / HISTORY

Sechs Tage langes, christliches Fest, das vor Anbruch der Fastenzeit gefeiert wird
A six-day Christian festival celebrated before the beginning of Lent

„Fastelovend"
niederdeutsch „Abend vor der Fastenzeit"
Low German for "evening before Lent"

„Carnevale"
Kurzform des kirchenlateinischen „carnislevamen" (Fleischwegnahme)
Short form of the Church Latin "carnislevamen" (farewell to meat)

KALENDER / CALENDAR

1 MITTWOCHNACHT / WEDNESDAY NIGHT
Hemdglunkerumzug und Einläuten der Fasnet
Hemdglunker procession and ringing in of Carnival

2 SCHMUTZIGE DUNNSCHDIG / FAT THURSDAY
Aufstellen des Narrenbaums, Übergabe des Rathausschlüssels, Fettgebackenes (Schmotz/Schmutz = Fett)
Erection of the fools' tree, handing over of the town hall key, deep-fried pastries (schmotz/dirt = fat)

3 FASNETFRITTIG / CARNIVAL FRIDAY
Suuressen, Hirnsuppe, Kutteln
Sour food, brain soup, tripe

4 FASNETSAMSCHDIG / CARNIVAL SATURDAY
Narrenfeste, Kinderfasnet
Fools' parties, children's carnival

5 FASNETSUNNDIG / CARNIVAL SUNDAY
Narrenfeste, Kinderumzüge
Fools' parties, children's parades

6 FASNETMÄNDIG / SHROVE MONDAY
Narrensprünge
Shrove Monday processions

7 FASNETZISCHDIG / CARNIVAL TUESDAY
Kehraus
Finale

8 ASCHERMITTWOCH / ASH WEDNESDAY
Beginn der Fastenzeit
Start of Lent

NARRENRUF / FOOLS' CALL
Es gibt verschiedene Narrenrufe. Der verbreitetste ist:
There are various fools' calls. The most common is:

„NARRI, NARRO"

TYPISCHE NARREN-UTENSILIE
TYPICAL FOOLS' UTENSILS

Fuchsschwanz
Foxtail

Klepperle
Noisemaker

Maske (Larve, Scheme)
Mask (larva)

Flecklehäs: Kostüm aus vielen bunten Stoffteilen
Flecklehäs: costume made of many colourful pieces of fabric

Saubloder (Schweinsblase)
Pig's bladder

Glocken, Schellen
Bells

Hexenbesen
Witch's broom

Rätsche
Ratchet

Strohschuhe
Straw shoes

DIE LARVEN / THE MASKS

Die Masken werden Larven genannt. Sie entlarven menschliche Eigenschaften. / The masks are called larvae. They expose (German: "entlarven") human traits.

Charakter- und Glattlarven / Character and smooth masks: **Morbili, Narrone, Gschell, Guller**

Grotesklarven / Grotesque masks: **Joggele, Pflumeschlucker, Fratz, Dengele**

Hexen- und Teufellarven / Witch and devil masks: **Hexe, Teufel, Federahannes, Spättlemadle**

Tierlarven / Animal masks: **Bär, Fuchs, Affe, Heuhopper**

Internationale Gäste
International guests

Wer die Ferienregion Schwarzwald besucht
Who visits the Black Forest holiday region

ca. 8,9 Mio. / mil.
Ankünfte pro Jahr
Arrivals per year

ca. 22,77 Mio. / mil.
Übernachtungen pro Jahr
Overnight stays per year

Betriebe mit >9 Betten
Accommodations >9 beds

ca. 56 Mio. / mil.
Übernachtungen pro Jahr
Overnight stays per year

Inkl. ca. 8000 Gastgeber und Privatvermieter mit weniger als 10 Betten, private und nicht gewerbliche Übernachtungen, Zweitwohnungen usw.
Incl. approx. 8,000 privately rented accommodations with fewer than 10 beds, private and non-commercial stays, second residences, etc.

2,6 Tage / 2.6 days
bleibt ein Gast durchschnittlich.
Average tourist stay

Wie die Gäste sich verteilen / Where do guests stay

NÖRDLICHER SCHWARZWALD
NORTHERN BLACK FOREST

 ca. 2,7 Mio. / mil. Ankünfte / Arrivals

 ca. 6,51 Mio. / mil. Übernachtungen / Overnight stays

 2,4 Tage / days Aufenthaltsdauer / Length of stay

MITTLERER SCHWARZWALD
CENTRAL BLACK FOREST

 ca. 2,54 Mio. / mil. Ankünfte / Arrivals

 ca. 6,06 Mio. / mil. Übernachtungen / Overnight stays

 2,4 Tage / days Aufenthaltsdauer / Length of stay

SÜDLICHER SCHWARZWALD
SOUTHERN BLACK FOREST

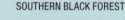

 ca. 3,65 Mio. / mil. Ankünfte / Arrivals

 ca. 10,2 Mio. / mil. Übernachtungen / Overnight stays

 2,8 Tage / days Aufenthaltsdauer / Length of stay

Woher die Gäste kommen / Where do guests come from

71,3 % Deutschland Germany	**10,1 %** Schweiz Switzerland	**4,1 %** Frankreich France	**3,3 %** Niederlande Netherlands	**1,3 %** Belgien Belgium	**1,0 %** Italien Italy	**0,9 %** Vereinigtes Königreich United Kingdom	**0,8 %** Spanien Spain	

0,8 % Österreich Austria	**0,7 %** USA	**0,6 %** China, Hongkong Hong Kong	**0,5 %** Luxemburg Luxembourg	**0,4 %** Arabische Golfstaaten Gulf States	**0,4 %** Israel	**0,4 %** Russland Russia	**3,4 %** Andere Others

ATTRAKTIONEN / ATTRAKTIONEN

LANDSCHAFT ERLEBEN / COUNTRYSIDE
- **Wutachschlucht** — Wutach Gorge
- **Markgräflerland**
- **Nationalpark Schwarzwald** — Black Forest National Park
- **Rheinauen** — Rhine floodplains – **Taubergießen**
- **Schauinsland**
- **2 Naturparks** — 2 Nature Parks
- **Donauquelle** — Source of the Danube, **Donaueschingen**
- **Kaiserstuhl**
- **Titisee**
- **Triberger Wasserfälle** — Triberg Waterfalls
- **Schluchsee**
- **Feldberg**
- **Biosphärengebiet Schwarzwald** — The Black Forest Biosphere Reserve
- **Belchen**

STÄDTE ERLEBEN / TOWNS
- **Bad Herrenalb**
- **Freiburg**
- **Bad Wildbad**
- **Baden-Baden**
- **Villingen-Schwenningen**
- **Schiltach**
- **Hausach**
- **Bad Liebenzell**
- **Offenburg**
- **Bad Teinach-Zavelstein**
- **Karlsruhe**
- **Bad Dürrheim**
- **Staufen**
- **Pforzheim**
- **Badenweiler**

MUSEEN ERLEBEN / MUSEUMS
- **Deutsches Tagebucharchiv** — German diary archive, **Emmendingen**
- **Schmuckmuseum** — Jewellery Museum, **Pforzheim**
- **Unimog-Museum, Gaggenau**
- **Heimatmuseum** — Heritage Museum, **Hüsli, Grafenhausen-Rothaus**
- **Winterhalter-Museum, Menzenschwand**
- **Auto- und Uhrenwelt** — Car and Timepiece Museum, **Schramberg**
- **Weltgrößte Kuckucksuhren** — Biggest cuckoo clocks in the world, **Triberg & Schonach**
- **Hans-Thoma-Museum, Bernau**
- **Vitra Design Museum, Weil am Rhein**
- **Besucherbergwerke** — visitor mines
- **Schwarzwälder Freilichtmuseum Vogtsbauernhof** — Black Forest Open Air Museum, **Gutach**
- **Hermann-Hesse-Museum, Calw**
- **Uhrenmuseum** — Clock Museum, **Furtwangen**
- **Schloss und ZKM (Zentrum für Kunst und Medien)** / Palace and ZKM (Center for Art and Media), **Karlsruhe**

FREIZEIT ERLEBEN / LEISURE
- **Sterne-Restaurants** — Starred restaurants, **Baiersbronn**
- **Europa-Park** — Amusement park, **Rust**
- **Staatsbrauerei** — Baden State Brewery **Rothaus**
- **Sauschwänzlebahn,** Wutach Valley Railway, **Blumberg**
- **ThyssenKrupp-Turm** — ThyssenKrupp Tower, **Rottweil**
- **Schwarzwald-Klinik, Glottertal**
- **Freizeitpark** — Theme park and zoo, **Steinwasen, Oberried**
- **Faller-Miniaturwelten** — Faller Miniature Worlds, **Gütenbach**
- **Galopprennbahn** — Racetrack, **Iffezheim**

KULTURDENKMÄLER ERLEBEN / CULTURAL HERITAGE
- **Größter Marktplatz Deutschlands** — Germany's largest market square, **Freudenstadt**
- **Barockresidenz** — Baroque residence, **Rastatt**
- **Weltgrößtes Adventskalenderhaus** — World's largest advent calendar house, **Gengenbach**
- **Kloster Alpirsbach** — Alpirsbach Abbey
- **Schloss Staufenberg** — Staufenberg Castle, **Durbach**
- **Freiburger Münster** — Freiburg Cathedral
- **Stephansmünster** — St. Steven's Cathedral, **Breisach**
- **Längste gedeckte Holzbrücke Europas** — Europe's longest covered wooden bridge, **Bad Säckingen**
- **Botanischer Garten Karlsruhe** — Karlsruhe Botanical Gardens
- **Schloss Donaueschingen** — Donaueschingen Palace

KULTUR ERLEBEN / CULTURAL EVENTS
- **Schlossfestspiele** — Castle Festival, **Ettlingen**
- **Stimmen-Festival** — Music Festival, **Lörrach**
- **Orgeln** / Organs, **Waldkirch**
- **Schuttig-Fasnet** — Carnival, **Elzach**
- **Donaueschinger Musiktage** — Donaueschingen Festival
- **Festspiele** — Festivals, **Baden-Baden**

Berühmte Gäste
Famous guests

Viele kommen für ein paar Tage, manche bleiben für immer.
Many come here for a few days, some stay on.

Ingo Appelt ★ Veronika Ferres ★ Jessica Alba ★ Deutsche Fußballnationalmannschaft / German national football team ⚽ Hannah Arendt ★ Fjodor Dostojewski ★ Konrad Adenauer ★ Rudi Michel ★ Wolfgang Ambros ★ Eros Ramazzotti ★ Horst Antes ★ Peter Maffay ★ Knut Hamsun ★ Mike Krüger ★ Georg Baselitz ★ Felix Mendelssohn Bartholdy ★ Alice Cooper ★ Hillary Clinton ★ Pierre Boulez ★ Karl Dall ★ Rudolf Schock ★ Marianne Birthler ★ Thomas Mann ★ Joe Bausch ★ Charles de Gaulle ★ Uwe Ochsenknecht ★ Bully Herbig ★ Heino Ferch ★ Katarina Barley ★ Joachim Gauck ★ Placido Domingo ★ Edmund Stoiber ★ Wolfgang Schüssel ★ Robert Koch ★ Ferdinand Porsche ★ Willy Brandt ★ Greta Garbo ★ Hector Berlioz ★ Anton Tschechow ★ Udo Jürgens ★ Johannes Brahms ★ Renate Schmidt ★ Scheich Ibn Saud ★ John Travolta ★ Max Brod ★ Thomas Berthold ★ Ferdinand Fürst von Bismarck ★ Werner Heisenberg ★ Leni Riefenstahl ★ Julian Nida-Rümelin ★ Marie Antoinette ★ Papst Benedikt XVI. ★ Max Schautzer ★ Rihanna ★ Emil Bizer ★ Werner Bergengruen ★ Günther Maria Halmer ★ Josephine Baker ★ Nena ★ Maxim Gorki ★ Hans-Dietrich Genscher ★ Natalia Wörner ★ Thomas Cook ★ Bülent Ceylan ★ Martin Heidegger ★ VfL Wolfsburg ⚽ Joe Cocker ★ Wolfgang Clement ★ Holger Börner ★ Helmut Markwort ★ Ursula Cantieni ★ Sven Ottke ★ Peter Dreher ★ Richard Wagner ★ Peter Lohmeyer ★ Eleonora Duse ★ Annemarie Renger ★ FC Schalke 04 ⚽ Walt Disney ★ Theodor Storm ★ Dalai Lama ★ Rainer Eppelmann ★ Elisabeth „Sisi" von Österreich ★ Josef Ertel ★ Fanta Vier ★ Otto Flake ★ Harold Faltermeyer ★ Rowan Atkinson ★ Jimi Hendrix ★ Karl Lagerfeld ★ Justus Frantz ★ Wilhelm Furtwängler ★ Mark Twain ★ Markus Bott ★ Isabelle Faust ★ Erasmus von Rotterdam ★ Volker Finke ★ Scholem Alejchem ★ Uschi Glas ★ Carl Bosch ★ Buffalo Bill ★ Meg Ryan ★ Christoffel von Grimmelshausen ★ Oskar Schlemmer ★ Nikolai Gogol ★ Karel Gott ★ Karl-Theodor zu Guttenberg ★ Roger Whittaker ★ Hans Baldung Grien ★ Gerhart Hauptmann ★ Hans Christian Andersen ★ Helene Fischer ★ Kaiser Wilhelm II. ★ Johannes Heesters ★ Nelly Furtado ★ Eva Herzigová ★ Friedrich August von Hayek ★ Robert Habeck ★ Bertolt Brecht ★ Ozzy Osbourne ★ Henry Ford ★ Olaf Scholz

> Nächstes Mal machen wir den Westweg.

> Habe bestimmt drei Kilo zugenommen.

> herz. erfrischend. echt. Echt jetzt.

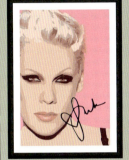

★ Per Kirkeby ★ Sarah Bernhardt ★ Christoph Maria Herbst ★ Maria Furtwängler ★ Hildegard Hamm-Brücher ★ Michelle Hunziker ★ Ulla Schmidt ★ Lars Riedel ★ Anna Netrebko ★ Amy Winehouse ★ Matthias Schweighöfer ★ Karl Hopfner ★ Jerry Hall ★ Johann Strauß ★ Mireille Mathieu ★ Roman Herzog ★ Whitney Houston ★ Paul Hindemith ★ Charles Regnier ★ Charles Huber ★ Gerhard Schröder ★ Kylie Minogue ★ Pink ★ Elijah Wood ★ Wangari Maathai ★ Walter Eucken ★ Alfred Döblin ★ Katarina Witt ★ Philipp Röth ★ Ernest Hemingway ★ Diane Krüger ★ Englische Fußballnationalmannschaft / England national football team ⚽ Albert Schweitzer ★ Edmund Husserl ★ Joshua Jackson ★ Peter Kraus ★ Wolfgang Thierse ★ Felix Kuby ★ Bruno Walter ★ Marcel Reif ★ Helmut Kohl ★ Chulalongkorn, King of Siam (Thailand) ★ Hussein bin Talal, King of Jordan ★ Marianne Koch ★ Konstantin Wecker ★ Niccolò Paganini ★ Markus Lüpertz ★ Hans Klok ★ Thomas Gottschalk ★ Klaus Theweleit ★ Annette Kolb ★ Erol Sander ★ Gustav Stresemann ★ Loriot ★ Ursula von der Leyen ★ Gabriele Wohmann ★ Stephan Balkenhol ★ Angela Merkel ★ Stefan Raab ★ Franz Liszt ★ Horst Lichter ★ Alexandra Maria Lara ★ Sepp Herberger ★ Jenny Lind ★ VfB Stuttgart ⚽ Max Beckmann ★ Lang Lang ★ Lothar de Maizière ★ Nelson Mandela ★ Helmut Schmidt ★ Gloria Fürstin von Thurn und Taxis ★ Karl Marx ★ Jürgen von der Lippe ★ Madonna ★ Indira Gandhi ★ Christian Neureuther ★ Miroslav Nemec ★ Christoph Meckel ★ Bernd Hölzenbein ★ Barack Obama ★ Tigran Petrosjan ★ Prinsesse Benedikte til Danmark ★ Oleg Popov ★ Luise von Preußen ★ TSG 1899 Hoffenheim ⚽ Walter Röhrl ★ Max Raabe ★ Johannes Rau ★ Daniel Roth ★ Sergei Wassiljewitsch Rachmaninow ★ Luise Rinser ★ Wolfgang Rihm ★ Clara Schumann ★ Nigel Kennedy ★ Bjarne Mädel ★ Heide Simonis ★ Sultan bin Muhammad Al-Qasimi ★ 1. FC Köln ⚽ Theodor Heuss ★ Rosi Mittermaier ★ Jutta Speidel ★ Jessica Stockmann ★ Sasha ★ Uwe Bein ★ Nicolas Sarkozy ★ René Schickele ★ Johannes Fürst von Thurn und Taxis ★ Iwan Turgenjew ★ Johann Wolfgang von Goethe ★ Lew Tolstoi ★ Rainer Trüby ★ Günther Verheugen ★ Victoria, Queen of the United Kingdom of Great Britain and Ireland, Empress of India ★ Wiener Sängerknaben ★ Carl-Friedrich Freiherr von Weizsäcker ★ Nike Wagner ★ Elmar Wepper ★ Alicia Keys ★ Helmut Zierl ★ Frank-Walter Steinmeier ★ Reinhold Beckmann ★ Marlene Dietrich ★ Florian David Fitz ★ Borussia Dortmund ⚽ Anton Rubinstein ★ Cees Nooteboom ★ Bill Clinton ★ Rainer Holzschuh ★ Olaf Schubert ★ Märtha Louise, Prinsesse av Norge ★ Silvia Van Zweden ★ Brasilianisches Fußballnationalteam / Brazil national football team ⚽

> Baden-Baden is so nice, you have to name it twice.

> Ich hätte doch eine Kuckucksuhr kaufen sollen …

> Come si dice „Auf Wiedersehen" in alemanno?

Wo schon die alten Römer badeten
Where the ancient Romans used to bathe

Heil- und Thermalbäder im Schwarzwald
Spas and thermal baths in the Black Forest

BERÜHMTE THERMEN UND BÄDER
FAMOUS SPAS AND BATHS

VITA CLASSICA THERME
Bad Krozingen
Thermenpartnerschaft mit Taketa in Japan
Partnership with the spa town of Taketa in Japan

CASSIOPEIA-THERME
Badenweiler
Hier wurden Anton Tschechow, Luise Rinser und Prinz Wilhelm von Preußen behandelt.
This is where Anton Chekhov, Luise Rinser and Prince Wilhelm of Prussia were treated.

In der Nachkriegszeit kommen Hunderttausende Gäste zur Kur in den Schwarzwald.
In the post-war period, hundreds of thousands of guests came to the Black Forest for treatment.

RADON REVITALBAD
St. Blasien-Menzenschwand
Baden in radonhaltigem Heilwasser in separaten Wannenbädern – nur auf ärztliche Verordnung!
Baths can be taken in healing, radon-containing water in separate tubs – only with a doctor's prescription!

BALINEA-THERME
Bad Bellingen
„Die Totes-Meer-Salzgrotte ist der ideale Ort, um nachhaltig zu entspannen."
"The Dead Sea Salt Grotto is the ideal place for lasting relaxation."

AQUALON-THERME
Bad Säckingen
Das Wasser im Naturbad ist unbeheizt und frei von Chlor und Chemie.
The water in the natural pool is unheated and free of chlorine and chemicals.

Gesundheitsreformen nach 1989 führen zu rapidem Besucherrückgang; Beispiel Bad Wildbad:
Health reforms after 1989 led to a rapid decline in visitors; for example in Bad Wildbad:

640.000
Gäste / guests
1981

163.000
Gäste / guests
2010

FRIEDRICHSBAD
Baden-Baden
2.000 Jahre alte römische Badruinen
2,000-year-old ruins of Roman baths

ALBTHERME
Waldbronn
Innen-, Außen-, Spaß- und Therapiebecken 30–35° C warm
Indoor, outdoor, play and therapy pools at 30–35° C

ROTHERMA
Gaggenau-Bad Rotenfels
Special: Felsensauna und Eisgrotte
Special attractions: rock sauna and ice grotto

SIEBENTÄLER-THERME
Bad Herrenalb
Liegt malerisch unter dem Falkensteinfelsen.
Picturesquely set at the foot of Falcon Rock.

Vor 2.000 Jahren legen römische Soldaten in Baden-Baden und Badenweiler Thermalanlagen an.
2,000 years ago, Roman soldiers built thermal baths in Baden-Baden and Badenweiler.

PALAIS THERMAL
Bad Wildbad
„Deutschlands sinnlichstes Sauna-& Thermalbad"
"Germany's most sensual sauna & thermal spa"

PARACELSUS-THERME
Bad Liebenzell
Das Außenbecken ist vom Schwarzwald umrankt.
The outdoor pool is ensconced in the Black Forest.

MINERALTHERME
Bad Teinach
Das kleinste Heilbad Baden-Württembergs
The smallest health spa in Baden-Württemberg

SOLEMAR
Bad Dürrheim
Aus Bad Dürrheim kommt ein Bio-Mineralwasser.
An organic mineral water comes from Bad Dürrheim.

Die legendäre *Schwarzwaldklinik* wurde in der Klinik Glotterbad der Landesversicherungsanstalt Württemberg gedreht. (1985–89, in TV)
The legendary *Schwarzwaldklinik* TV show was shot at the Glotterbad Clinic run by the Württemberg State Social Insurance Agency.

Nah bei Gott
Nearer My God to Thee

Klöster, Kirchen und andere Gotteshäuser
Monasteries, churches and other places of worship

NEUSTÄDTER MÜNSTER / ST. JAMES' MINSTER

Das Münster heißt Münster, obwohl es eigentlich eine Pfarrkirche ist.
This minster is actually a parish church.

FRIDOLINSMÜNSTER / ST. FRIDOLIN'S MINSTER, Bad Säckingen

Unterschiedlich hohe Türme: 55,80 m und 55,70 m
Towers of different heights: 55.80 and 55.70 m

KLOSTER MAULBRONN / MAULBRONN MONASTERY

Die Vorhalle der Klosterkirche wird auch „Paradies" genannt.
The porch of the monastery church is also known as "Paradise".

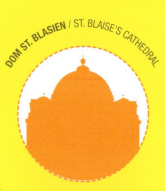

DOM ST. BLASIEN / ST. BLAISE'S CATHEDRAL

Die Kuppel des „Schwarzwälder Doms" ist mit 36 m Spannweite eine der größten in Europa.
The dome of the "Black Forest Cathedral" is one of the largest in Europe with a span of 36 m.

WALLFAHRTSKIRCHE UNSERER LIEBEN FRAU / SANCTUARY OF OUR LADY, Todtmoos

Dietrich von Rickenbach lässt 1255 eine Kapelle errichten, nachdem er die giftigen Dämpfe im „toten Moos" bezwungen hatte.
Dietrich von Rickenbach had a chapel built in 1255 after conquering the toxic fumes of the "dead moss".

FREIBURGER MÜNSTER / FREIBURG CATHEDRAL

„Der schönste Turm der Christenheit" (Jacob Burckhardt, Kunsthistoriker). Es hat noch niemand widersprochen.
"The most beautiful tower in Christendom" (Jacob Burckhardt, art historian). No one has ever tried to deny it.

KLOSTER ALPIRSBACH / ALPIRSBACH ABBEY

Maximilian I. (1459–1519), Erzherzog von Österreich, König und Kaiser des Heiligen Römischen Reichs Deutscher Nation, nächtigt mehrfach im Kloster.
Maximilian I (1459–1519), Archduke of Austria, King and Emperor of the Holy Roman Empire of the German Nation, spent several nights at the abbey.

STADTKIRCHE FREUDENSTADT / FREUDENSTADT CITY CHURCH

Das 120 cm hohe, aus einem Stück geschnitzte Lesepult ist eines der bedeutendsten Holzbildwerke des 12. Jh.s.
The lectern, 120 cm high and carved from a single piece of wood, is one of the most important wooden sculptures of the 12th century.

SYNAGOGE FREIBURG / FREIBURG SYNAGOGUE

Ein Mahnmal vor der Universität erinnert an die alte, 1938 von der SA niedergebrannte Synagoge.
A memorial in front of the university commemorates the old synagogue, burned down by Nazi storm troopers in 1938.

STEPHANSMÜNSTER / ST. STEVEN'S CATHEDRAL, Breisach

Über 100 m² großes Wandgemälde „Das Jüngste Gericht" von Martin Schongauer
Mural painting of "The Last Judgement" by Martin Schongauer, measuring over 100 sqm

KLOSTER ST. TRUDPERT / ST. TRUDPERT'S ABBEY, Münstertal

Um 600 n. Chr. versucht der iroschottische Mönch Trudpert, die heidnischen Alemannen zu missionieren.
Circa 600 AD the Celtic monk Trudpert tried to convert the pagan Alemanni.

KLOSTER ST. MÄRGEN / ABBEY OF ST. MÄRGEN

Das Klostermuseum zeigt nicht Kloster-, sondern Schwarzwälder Uhrengeschichte.
The abbey museum is devoted to the history not of the abbey but of Black Forest clocks.

ZENTRALMOSCHEE / CENTRAL MOSQUE, Offenburg

2013 kippt bei Bauarbeiten das Minarett um und wird 2015 durch ein neues ersetzt.
The minaret toppled over during construction work in 2013 and was replaced in 2015.

ST. PETER UND PAUL / CHURCH OF STS. PETER & PAUL, St. Peter

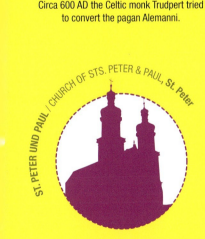

Die Bibliothek besitzt eine Koberger-Bibel von 1483, eine Erstausgabe von *Utopia* von Thomas Morus und ein Markusblatt vom Ende des 10. Jh.s.
The library owns a Koberg Bible from 1483, a first edition of Thomas More's *Utopia* and a St. Mark manuscript from the end of the 10th century.

KLOSTER HIRSAU / HIRSAU ABBEY

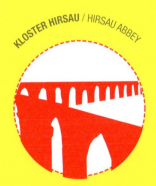

Der Abt beschwert sich 1570 bei der herzoglichen Kanzlei in Stuttgart, dass seine Schüler bis nach Mitternacht für die Kirchenräte singen müssen.
In 1570 the abbot complained to the ducal chancellery in Stuttgart that his pupils had to sing for the church councillors until after midnight.

AUTOBAHNKIRCHE ST. CHRISTOPHORUS / MOTORWAY CHURCH OF ST. CHRISTOPHER, Baden-Baden

Jährlich ca. 300.000 Besucher, nach dem Freiburger Münster meistbesuchte Kirche im Erzbistum Freiburg
With around 300,000 visitors annually, second only to Freiburg Cathedral as the most frequented church in the Archdiocese of Freiburg

Ein Heiliger im Schwarzwald
A saint in the Black Forest

Das Longinuskreuz – eine Sonderform der Arma-Christi-Kreuze – gibt es fast nur im Schwarzwald. / The Longinus cross, a special form of the Arma Christi cross, is found almost exclusively in the Black Forest.

WOFÜR DIE GEGENSTÄNDE STEHEN
WHAT THE OBJECTS STAND FOR

Hahn: Verleugnung Christi durch Petrus
Rooster: Peter's denial of Christ

Rutenbündel: Geißelung Jesu
Flagellum: the flagellation of Jesus

Geldbeutel oder Silberlinge: Judaslohn
Purse/pieces of silver: the reward for Judas' betrayal

Leichenhemd
Shroud

Schädel: Begräbnis auf Golgatha
Skull: burial on Golgotha

Zange: zum Lösen der Nägel vom Kreuz
Pincers: to remove the nails from the cross

Würfel: Römische Soldaten spielten um Jesu Rock.
Dice: Roman soldiers cast lots for Jesus' robe

Laterne: die Gefangennahme bei Nacht
Lantern: the arrest at night

Lilie: die Auferstehung von den Toten
Lily: resurrection from the dead

Dornenkrone
Crown of thorns

Kreuznägel
Nails

Schweißtuch: reicht Veronika Jesus
Veil of Veronica: used to wipe Jesus' face

Hammer
Hammer

Fesseln: Jesu Gefangennahme
Cords/chains: used to bind Jesus

Purpurrock
Purple robe of mockery

Essigschwamm, der Jesus gereicht wurde
Vinegar sponge handed to Jesus

Kanne und Waschschüssel: Handwaschung des Pilatus
Vessel and washbowl: Pilate washing his hands

Abendmahlkelch: Kelch, mit dem Josef von Arimathäa Jesu Blut auffing
Holy Grail: chalice in which Joseph of Arimathea caught Jesus' blood

Untergewand Jesu
Jesus' undergarment

Hand: die Hand Gottes
Hand: the hand of God

Leiter: Abnahme Jesu vom Kreuz
Ladder: Deposition from the cross

Jesus am Kreuz mit den fünf Wundmalen ist umrankt von bis zu 25 Gegenständen, die seine Passionsgeschichte erzählen.
Jesus on the cross with the five stigmata is surrounded by up to 25 objects that tell the story of the Passion.

Longinus war der römische Centurio, der Jesus eine Lanze in die Seite stach.
Longinus was the Roman centurion who stabbed Jesus in the side with a lance.

Er erkannte: „Wahrhaft, dies war Gottes Sohn!"
He realised: "Truly, this was the Son of God!"

Eine Stadt geht zu Bruch
A town falls to pieces

In Staufen haben die Häuser Risse bekommen.
The houses in Staufen have developed cracks.

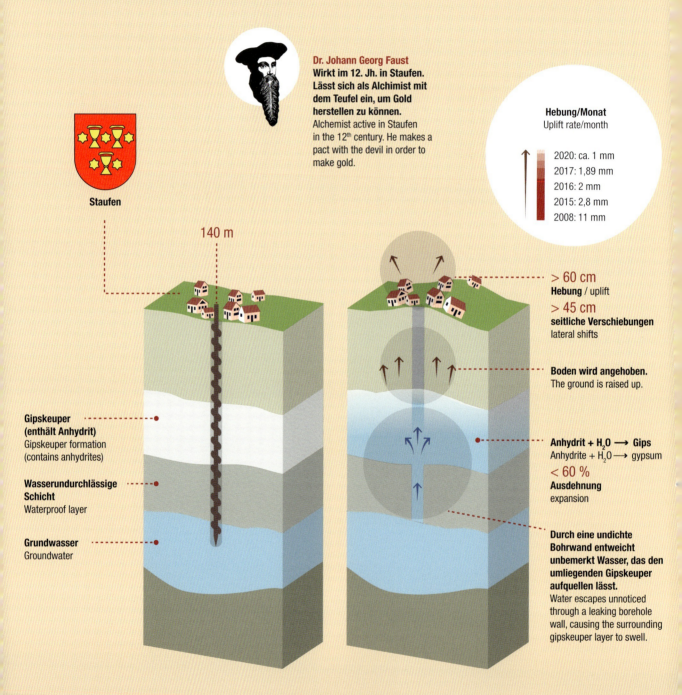

Dr. Johann Georg Faust
Wirkt im 12. Jh. in Staufen. Lässt sich als Alchimist mit dem Teufel ein, um Gold herstellen zu können.
Alchemist active in Staufen in the 12th century. He makes a pact with the devil in order to make gold.

Staufen

Hebung/Monat
Uplift rate/month

2020: ca. 1 mm
2017: 1,89 mm
2016: 2 mm
2015: 2,8 mm
2008: 11 mm

140 m

Gipskeuper (enthält Anhydrit)
Gipskeuper formation (contains anhydrites)

Wasserundurchlässige Schicht
Waterproof layer

Grundwasser
Groundwater

> 60 cm
Hebung / uplift

> 45 cm
seitliche Verschiebungen
lateral shifts

Boden wird angehoben.
The ground is raised up.

Anhydrit + H$_2$O → Gips
Anhydrite + H$_2$O → gypsum

< 60 %
Ausdehnung
expansion

Durch eine undichte Bohrwand entweicht unbemerkt Wasser, das den umliegenden Gipskeuper aufquellen lässt.
Water escapes unnoticed through a leaking borehole wall, causing the surrounding gipskeuper layer to swell.

September / September
2007
Bohrung von sieben tiefen Geothermiesonden unter dem historischen Rathaus zur Nutzung von Erdwärme
Drilling of seven geothermal probes under the historic town hall to tap geothermal energy

Oktober / October
2007
Gebäude in einem Umkreis von 500 Metern bekommen Risse. Bodenheizungen fallen aus, Treppen verziehen sich, Fenster zersplittern, Häuser spalten sich …
Buildings within a radius of 500 metres develop cracks. Floor heating fails, stairs warp, windows shatter, houses split …

Bis / Until
2009
Hebungsgeschwindigkeit: 11 mm/Monat
Uplift rate: 11 mm/month

Bis April / Until April
2007
Bau von Abwehrbrunnen zur Grundwasserabsenkung führen zur Reduzierung der Hebungsgeschwindigkeit.
Construction of entrapment wells to lower the groundwater level leads to a reduction in the rate of uplift.

August / August
2013
Das Schlossberg-Wäscherei-Haus muss abgerissen werden.
The Schlossberg laundry building must be demolished.

ca. 270
Gebäude rund um Rathausplatz beschädigt
buildings all around Rathausplatz damaged

Staufen darf nicht zerbrechen!

September / September
2014
Das rückwärtige Rathausgebäude wird teilabgerissen.
The rear town hall building is partially torn down.

2020
Hebungsgeschwindigkeit hat sich auf max. 1 mm/Monat reduziert.
Uplift rate has been reduced to max. 1 mm/month.

Bis / Until
2020
ca. 50.000.000 € Sachschaden
in property damage

Bahnbrechende Tüftler
Trailblazing tinkerers

Schwarzwälder, die die Welt veränderten
Black Forest inhabitants who changed the world

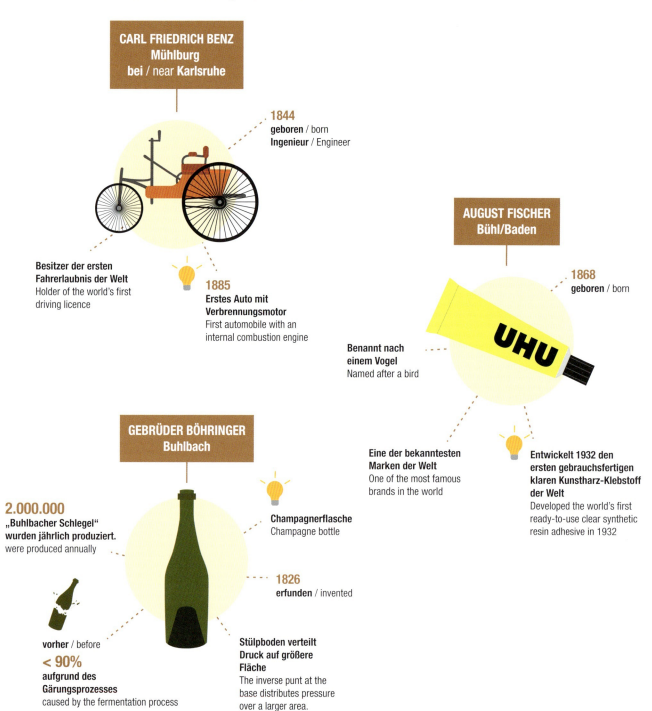

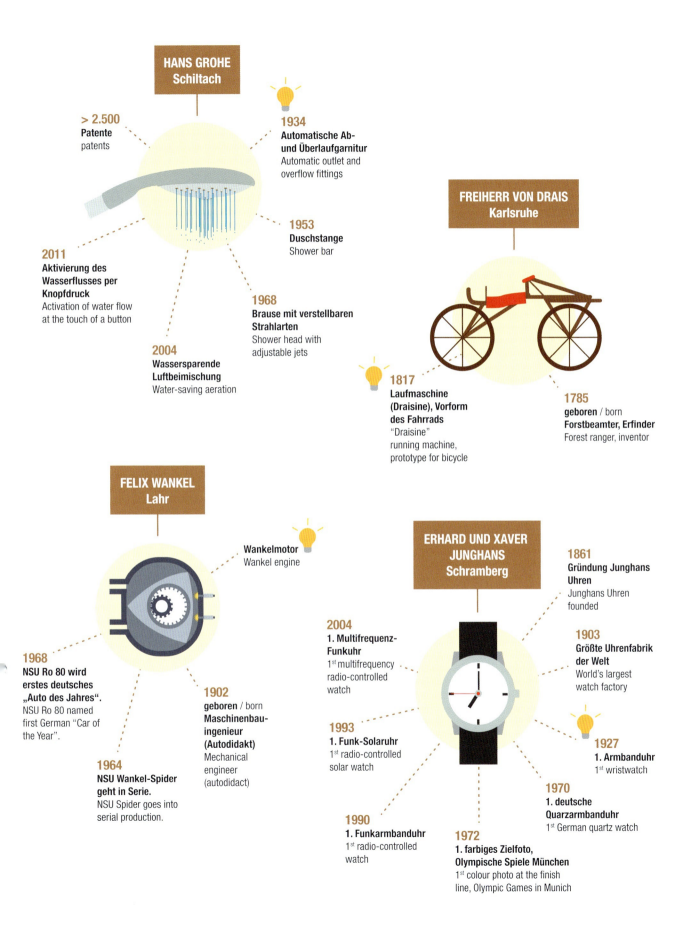

Die Allerbesten
The best of the best

Schwarzwälder Weltmarktführer / World market leaders from the Black Forest

Häfele
Nagold
Bau- und Möbelbeschläge
Furniture fittings and architectural hardware

Ekato
Freiburg
Rühr- und Mischtechnik
Agitation and mixing technology

Sick AG
Waldkirch
Logistikautomation, Prozessautomation, Sensorlösungen für die Industrie
Logistics automation, process automation, sensor solutions for industry

Hermetic-Pumpen
Gundelfingen
Hermetische Kreiselpumpen
Hermetic pumps

Zahoransky AG
Todtnau-Geschwend
Maschinen zur Fertigung von Zahnbürsten und Bürsten
Machines for automated brush production

Testo
Lenzkirch
Smarte Testgeräte
Smart test equipment

Stratec SE
Birkenfeld
Diagnostische Analysesysteme
Diagnostic analyser systems

Sonotronic Nagel
Karlsbad-Ittersbach
Ultraschall-Technologie für Autoindustrie
Ultrasonic technology for the automotive industry

Papierfabrik August Koehler
Oberkirch
Thermopapiere (Kassenzettel …)
Thermal paper (receipts, etc.)

Katz
Weisenbach
Bierdeckel
Beer coasters

Dr. Willmar Schwabe
Karlsruhe
pflanzliche Arzneimittel
Plant-based pharmaceuticals

IKA-Werke
Staufen
Labor-, Analyse- und Prozesstechnik-Maschinen
Laboratory equipment, analytical and process technologies

Hugo Kern und Liebers
Schramberg
Draht- und Bandfedern
Strip and wire parts and assemblies

Robert Bürkle
Freudenstadt
Pressen- und Beschichtungsanlagen für die Möbel-, Holz- und Bauindustrie
Presses and coating lines for surfaces for the furniture, woodworking and construction industries

Fischer Dübel
Waldachtal
Befestigungssysteme, Dübel, Schrauben …
Fixing systems, screws and plugs

Heinzmann
Schönau
Regelungs-, Steuerungs- und Abgasnachbehandlungslösungen für industrielle Verbrennungsmotoren und Turbinen
Regulation, control and exhaust aftertreatment solutions for industrial combustion engines and turbines

Gebr. Schmid
Freudenstadt
Automationssysteme für Fotovoltaikindustrie
Automation systems for the photovoltaic industry

Arburg
Loßburg
Spritzgießmaschinen für die Kunststoffverarbeitung
Injection moulding machine for plastics processing

Herrenknecht
Schwanau
Tunnelvortriebstechnik
Tunnelling systems

PTV
Karlsruhe
Mobilitäts-Planungs-Software
Mobility planning software

Polytec
Waldbronn
Optische Messsysteme, berührungslose Schwingungsmesstechnik
Optical measurement technology, non-contact vibration measurement

asknet
Karlsruhe
Outsourcing-Lösungen für den globalen Onlinevertrieb von Software
Outsourcing solutions for global online software distribution

Kasto
Achern
Industriesägen
Industrial saws

Witzenmann
Pforzheim
Metallschläuche, Kompensatoren, Metallbälge und Fahrzeugteile
Flexible metal pipe elements: expansion joints, metal bellows, automotive parts

 Jahresumsatz Annual turnover **> 50.000.000 €**

davon Ausland thereof abroad **mind. / at least 50 %**

In mind. 3 von 6 Kontinenten tätig Active on at least 3 of 6 continents

KNF Neuberger
Freiburg
Membranpumpen
Diaphragm pumps

 Nr. 1 oder Nr. 2 im betreffenden Weltmarkt(segment)
No. 1 or no. 2 in the relevant world market (segment)

Die Kunst der Stunde
A prime destination for art lovers

Im Schwarzwald gibt es viele bedeutende Museen und Kunstsammlungen.
The Black Forest boasts many important museums and art collections.

STAATLICHE KUNSTHALLE
Karlsruhe

Albrecht Dürer
Das Rhinozeros / The Rhinoceros

Rembrandt
Selbstbildnis / Self-portrait

Edgar Degas
Junge Tänzerin im Gegenlicht
Young Dancer Standing

August Macke
Leute am blauen See
People at the Blue Lake

ZKM
ZENTRUM FÜR KUNST UND MEDIEN
CENTER FOR ART AND MEDIA
Karlsruhe

Nam June Paik
Buddha

BADISCHES LANDESMUSEUM
Karlsruhe

Hans Baldung Grien
Schmerzensmann
Man of Sorrows

SCHMUCKMUSEUM
JEWELLERY MUSEUM
Pforzheim

Schlangenarmreif / Snake bracelet

AUGUSTINERMUSEUM
Freiburg

Matthias Grünewald
Das Schneewunder
Miracle of the Snow

Hermann Dischler
Wintermorgen im Schwarzwald
Winter Morning in the Black Forest

MUSEUM FRIEDER BURDA
Baden-Baden

Gerhard Richter
Kerze / Candle

MUSEUM FÜR NEUE KUNST
Freiburg

Peter Dreher
Tag um Tag guter Tag *
Day by Day, Good Day *

KUNSTHALLE MESSMER
Riegel am Kaiserstuhl

Ai WeiWei
Rock

HANS-THOMA-KUNSTMUSEUM
Bernau

Hans Thoma
Felsige Schwarzwaldhöhe
Rocky Slope in the Black Forest

* Dreher malt seit 1974 jeden Tag das gleiche Motiv: ein Glas / Dreher has been painting the same motif every day since 1974: a glass

VITRA DESIGN MUSEUM
Weil am Rhein

Charles & Ray Eames
DKW-1

KUNSTRAUM GRÄSSLIN
St. Georgen

Martin Kippenberger
Familie Hunger / Hunger Family

Imi Knoebel
19.09.2014

STÄDTISCHE GALERIE
Offenburg

Gretel Haas-Gerber
Ich und die Welt / Self-portrait

Die Fürstenmaler
The painter brothers

Franz Xaver und Hermann Fidel Winterhalter malten im 19. Jahrhundert alles, was Rang und Namen hatte. / In the nineteenth century, Franz Xaver and Hermann Fidel Winterhalter were celebrated portrait painters to the rich and royals.

ab / from ca. 1822
Studium der Malerei an der Kunstakademie München
Painting studies at the Munich Art Academy

ab / from 1828
Zeichenlehrer am Badischen Hof in Karlsruhe
Drawing teacher at the Baden Court in Karlsruhe

1833/34
Italienreise
Trip to Italy

Mittellose Bauernsöhne
Poor farmer's sons

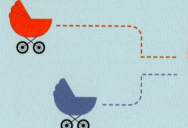

20. April 1805
Franz Xaver Winterhalter
Menzenschwand

23. September 1808
Hermann Fidel Winterhalter
Menzenschwand

Dorfschule in St. Blasien
Village school in St. Blasien

Studienaufenthalte in München und Rom
Study visits to Munich and Rome

ab / from 1818
Ausbildung am Herderschen Kunstinstitut in Freiburg
Art training at Herdersches Kunstinstitut in Freiburg

Königin
Charlotte von Belgien

Großherzogin
Sophie von Baden

Maria Karolina Augusta von Neapel-Sizilien

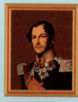
König
Leopold I.
von Belgien

Kaiserin
Elisabeth „Sisi"
von Österreich

Kaiser
Napoleon III.
von Frankreich

König
Louis-Phillipe
von Frankreich

1834
Ernennung zum
Großherzoglichen
Hofmaler
Appointed Grand Ducal
Court Painter

Umzug nach Paris
Moves to Paris.

1837
1. Preis beim
Pariser Salon
1st prize at
the Paris Salon

**Sie bereisen als
Porträtmaler ganz Europa.**
The portrait painters
travel all over Europe.

**8. Juli 1873
Frankfurt am Main**

**24. Februar 1891
Karlsruhe**

1840
Folgt seinem
Bruder nach Paris.
Follows his brother
to Paris.

Königin Isabella von Spanien
Leonilla Fürstin zu Sayn-Wittgenstein
Maximilian von Österreich
Kaiserin Eugenie von Frankreich
Großfürstin Olga von Württemberg
Kaiser Pedro II. von Brasilien
Königin Olga von Württemberg
Prinzessin Charlotte von Belgien
Prinzessin Mathilde Bonaparte
Edward Prinz von Sachsen-Weimar-Eisenach

Königin
Marie Christine
von Spanien

Königin
Victoria von England

Varvara
Rimsky-Korsakov

Königin
Marie Amelie
von Frankreich

Kaiser
Franz Joseph I.
von Österreich

Prinzessin
Cantacuzène
von Rumänien

Prinzessin
Charlotte
von Belgien

Gedächtnis einer Nation
Collective memory of a nation

Im Barbarastollen am Schauinsland, Europas größtem Archiv zur Langzeitarchivierung, lagert (fast) das gesamte deutsche Kulturgut auf Mikrofilm. / In the Barbarastollen on Schauinsland mountain, Europe's largest long-term archive, (nearly) all of German cultural heritage is stored on microfilm.

Einziges Objekt der BRD unter Sonderschutz lt. Haager Konvention
Only object in the Federal Republic of Germany under special protection by the Hague Convention

Oberried bei / near Freiburg

LAGERMENGE / QUANTITY STORED

 1.600 Edelstahl-Behälter / stainless steel containers

 ≈ **33.792 km** Mikrofilm / of microfilm

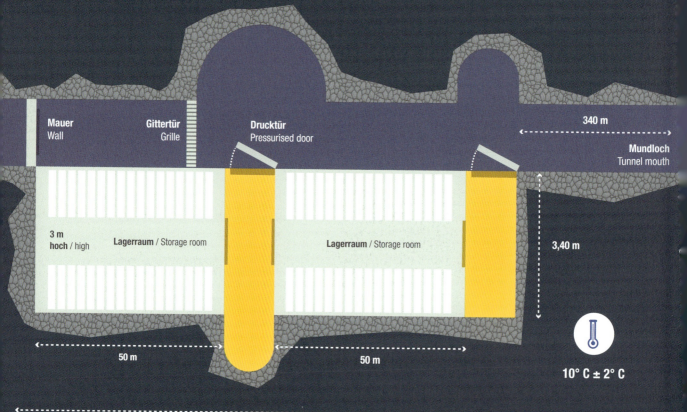

LUFTDICHTE V2A-EDELSTAHL-BEHÄLTER
AIRTIGHT V2A STAINLESS STEEL CONTAINERS

200 m
Granit und Gneis
Granite and gneiss

♦ 907
✚ 908

78 cm

43 cm

ca. 122 kg

16
Mikrofilmrollen
microfilm reels

1.320 m
Mikrofilm / of microfilm

1 m   33
Mikrofilm ≈ Aufnahmen
of microfilm   images

MIKROFILMAUFNAHMEN UNTER ANDEREM VON:
MICROFILM RECORDS INCLUDING:

Urkunde Kaiser Karls des Großen zugunsten des Regensburger Klosters St. Emmeram von 794
Royal charter issued by Charlemagne in 794 for St. Emmeram's Abbey in Regensburg

Bannandrohungsbulle von Papst Leo X. gegen Martin Luther von 1520
Papal bull issued by Pope Leo X in 1520 threatening Martin Luther with excommunication

Baupläne des Kölner Doms
Construction plans for Cologne Cathedral

Filmbestände der DDR
East German film stocks

Handschriften von Johann Sebastian Bach
Manuscripts written by Johann Sebastian Bach

Ernennungsurkunde von Adolf Hitler zum Reichskanzler
Certificate of appointment for Adolf Hitler as Reich Chancellor

Garant für gute Quoten
Good ratings guaranteed

Der Schwarzwald auf der Bühne, der Leinwand und der Mattscheibe / The Black Forest on stage, screen and TV.

Das kalte Herz / Heart of Stone

Spielfilm / Feature film (1922/23)
Die Innenaufnahmen wurden in Berlin gedreht.
The indoor scenes were shot in Berlin.

Stummfilm / Silent film (1930)
Gilt als verschollen.
Considered lost.

Kinderfilm, WDR
Children's film (1978)
Drehorte: Freilichtmuseum Vogtsbauernhof, Wildgehege Hellenthal
Filming locations: Vogtsbauernhof open-air museum, Hellenthal game reserve

Kinofilm DDR / Cine film GDR (1950)
Drehorte: DEFA-Studios in Potsdam-Babelsberg, Thüringen und Sachsen-Anhalt
Filming locations: DEFA studios in Potsdam-Babelsberg, Thuringia and Saxony-Anhalt

Spielfilm
Feature film (1933)
Drehorte: Berlin, Dolomiten, Tessin, Comer See, Schwarzwald
Filming locations: Berlin, Dolomites, Ticino, Lake Como, Black Forest

Fernsehserie, ZDF / TV series (1978/79)
Drehorte: Iberger Tropfsteinhöhle, Berlin. 6 Teile
Filming locations: Iberg stalactite cave, Berlin. 6 parts

TV-Film / Made-for-TV movie (2014)
Drehorte: Erdmannshöhle Hasel, Elendslöchle im Hännemer Wald, Solfelsen in Rickenbach, Elsass
Filming locations: Erdmannshöhle cave in Hasel, Elendslöchle canyon in Hännemer Forest, Solfelsen rock in Rickenbach, Alsace

Kinofilm / Cine film (2016)
Drehorte: Sachsen, Potsdam-Babelsberg, Wuppertal, Loßburg und Schluchsee
Filming locations: Saxony, Potsdam-Babelsberg, Wuppertal, Lossburg and Schluchsee

Märchen von Wilhelm Hauff, spielt im Schwarzwald
Fairy tale by Wilhelm Hauff, set in the Black Forest

OPERETTE / OPERETTA

Schwarzwaldmädel
(Black Forest Girl) (1917)
von Léon Jessel und August Neidhart;
UA: Komische Oper, Berlin
by Léon Jessel and August Neidhart; world premiere: Komische Oper, Berlin

KINOFILME / CINEMA

Schwarzwaldmädel
(The Black Forest Girl) (1950)
Verfilmung der Operette von Jessel und Neidhart, 1. Farbfilm nach 2. Weltkrieg,
> 16 Millionen Zuschauer
Film adaptation of the operetta by Jessel and Neidhart, 1st colour film made after the Second World War, >16 million viewers

Die Mühle im Schwarzwälder Tal (1953)
„Ländliches Nachkriegsdrama ohne die Landschaftsshow-Effekte sonstiger Heimatfilme." (Filmdienst)
"Post-war rural drama without the showy landscape effects of other Heimat films." (Filmdienst)

Schwarzwaldmelodie (1956)
UA: Stuttgarter Zoo Wilhelma
World premiere: Wilhelma Zoo in Stuttgart

Die Rosel vom Schwarzwald (1956)
Rosel wird zur „Miss Kirschwasser" gekürt.
Rosel is crowned "Miss Kirschwasser".

Das Posthaus im Schwarzwald (1958)
Regisseur Rudolf Schündler spielte den Diener in „Der Exorzist" und den Bürgermeister in „Michel muss mehr Männchen machen".
Director Rudolf Schündler played the servant in "The Exorcist" and the mayor in "New Mischief by Emil".

Schwarzwälder Kirsch (1958)
Drehorte: St. Peter, Titisee, Staufen, Freiburg und im Wiesental (außen), Ufa-Atelier, Berlin-Tempelhof (innen)
Filming locations: St. Peter, Titisee, Staufen, Freiburg and the Wiesental valley (outdoor scenes), Ufa Studio, Berlin-Tempelhof (indoor scenes)

Jules et Jim (1962)
Regie: François Truffaut. Jules verliebt sich in Catherine und zieht mit ihr in den Schwarzwald. Diese Szenen wurden im Elsass gedreht.
Director: François Truffaut. Jules falls in love with Catherine and moves to the Black Forest with her. But the scenes were shot in Alsace.

Schwarzwaldfahrt aus Liebeskummer (1974)
Roy Black singt „Hoch auf dem gelben Wagen" und andere Schlager.
Roy Black sings the folk song "Up on the Yellow Wagon" and other hits.

TV / TV

Schwarzwaldklinik
(1984–1988, 1991, 2005)
Fernsehserie, pro Folge bis zu 28 Millionen Zuschauer, 60 % Marktanteil. Lief in über 38 Ländern.
TV series, as many as 28 million viewers per episode, 60% market share. Shown in over 38 countries.

Die Fallers (seit / since 1994)
Die SWR-Schwarzwaldserie, über 1000 Folgen
The Black Forest series from the SWR public broadcasting network, over 1,000 episodes

Tatort Freiburg (seit / since 2016)
Fernsehkrimi aus Freiburg, der Stadt mit einer der höchsten Kriminalitätsraten Baden-Württembergs
TV crime thriller from Freiburg, the city with one of the highest crime rates in Baden-Württemberg

Tatort Schwarzwald (seit / since 2017)
Fernsehkrimi: Die Ermittler werden von gebürtigen Schwaben dargestellt. Eva Löbau (Hauptkommissarin Franziska Tobler) ist in Waiblingen geboren, Hans-Jochen Wagner (Hauptkommissar Friedemann Berg) in Tübingen.
TV crime thriller: The investigators are played by native Swabians. Eva Löbau (Chief Commissioner Franziska Tobler) was born in Waiblingen, Hans-Jochen Wagner (Chief Commissioner Friedemann Berg) in Tübingen.

Die Toten vom Schwarzwald (2010)
„‚Mystery' ist, wenn Logik fehlt." (Focus)
"'Mystery' is what you call it when there is no logic to the events." (Focus).

Es war einmal
Once upon a time

Schwarzwald zum Nachlesen
The Black Forest in literature and legend

"O Schwarzwald, o Heimat, wie bist du so schön"

1873 schrieb der Pforzheimer Unternehmer Ludwig Auerbach das Gedicht, das von Franz Abt vertont und zum Welthit wurde.
Ludwig Auerbach, a businessman from Pforzheim, wrote a poem in 1873 which, set to music by Franz Abt, became a world hit.

Der Pfarrer aus dem Wiesental schrieb als Erster auf Alemannisch.
The pastor from Wiesental Valley was the first to write in Alemannic.

1564 will Hornberg den Herzog von Württemberg mit Kanonenschüssen begrüßen. Als sich eine Staubwolke nähert, wird alles Pulver verschossen – es ist aber nur eine Postkutsche. Als der Herzog Stunden später eintrifft, ist kein Pulver mehr da.
In 1564 Hornberg decided to greet the Duke of Württemberg with a cannon salute. When a cloud of dust betrayed the approach of the Duke's carriage, the cannons went off – but it was only a post coach. When the Duke finally arrived, no gun powder was left.

Das Hornberger Schießen

SCHWARZWALDGESCHICHTEN / BLACK FOREST TALES

- Johann Peter Hebel **Alemannische Gedichte** — 1803
- Heinrich Hansjakob **Waldleute** — 1897
- Nicolai R. Østgaard **Drei Tage im Schwarzwald. Reiseschilderung eines norwegischen Advokaten und Stortingabgeordneten ...** — 1856
- Berthold Auerbach **Schwarzwälder Dorfgeschichten** — 1843–1854

MÄRCHEN, SAGEN ... / FAIRY TALES, LEGENDS ...

- **Die Mummelsee-Sage**
- **Das Seemännlein im Glaswaldsee**
- Wilhelm Hauff **Das kalte Herz** — 1827
- Joseph Victor von Scheffel **Der Trompeter von Säckingen** — 1854

ROMANE / NOVELS

- Jussi Adler-Olsen **Das Alphabethaus** — 1997
- Thommie Bayer **Einsam, zweisam, dreisam** — 1993
- Peter Gaymann **Typisch Badisch: Von Titisee bis Tuniberg** — 2015
- Hermann Hesse **Narziß und Goldmund** — 1930
- Hermann Hesse **Demian** — 1919
- Harald Hurst **Do hanne numm** — 2010
- Jens Schäfer **Umzugsroman** — 2008
- Arnold Stadler **Mein Hund, meine Sau, mein Leben** — 1994
- Gabriele Wohmann **Frühherbst in Badenweiler** — 1978
- Leonid Borissowitsch Zypkin **Ein Sommer in Baden-Baden** — 1982

Code Napoléon / Napoleonic Code
Die erste deutschsprachige Ausgabe erschien 1806 in Karlsruhe.
The first German edition was published in 1806 in Karlsruhe.

SCHWARZWALDKRIMIS UND -THRILLER (AUSWAHL) / BLACK FOREST CRIME NOVELS AND THRILLERS (A SELECTION)

Sanne Aswald	**Tod in der Ortenau**	2016
Daniel Oliver Bachmann	**Die Tote im Tann**	2018
Bert Dillert	**Der dunkle Schatten des Waldes**	2018
Ralf H. Dorweiler	**Mord auf Alemannisch**	2016
Ralf H. Dorweiler	**Schwarzwälder Schinken**	2016
Ralf H. Dorweiler	**Badische Blutsbrüder**	2016
Thomas Erle	**Teufelskanzel**	2013
Thomas Erle	**Höllsteig**	2015
Mona Franz	**Schwarzwälder Kirsch**	2020
Edi Graf	**Wolfsgebiet**	2019
Eva Klingler	**Schwarzwaldruh**	2015
Ralf Kühling	**Der Tote vom Schwarzwald**	2019
Manuela Kusterer	**Das Schweigen im Schwarzwald**	2018
Bernd Leix	**Schwarzwaldhölle**	2016
Bernd Leix	**Schwarzwaldhimmel**	2018
Christa S. Lotz	**Martinsmorde**	2018
Christa S. Lotz	**Tod am schwarzen Fluss**	2019
Ernst Obermaier	**Mörderischer Schwarzwald**	2017
Alexander Rieckhoff/Stefan Ummenhofer	**Narrentreiben**	2013
Alexander Rieckhoff/Stefan Ummenhofer	**Narrentreiben Schwarzwaldstrand**	2013
Alexander Rieckhoff/Stefan Ummenhofer	**Narrentreiben Schwarzwaldrauch**	2015
Chris Thame	**Schwarzwald. Blutrot**	2020
Ute Wehrle	**Schwarzwald sehen und sterben**	2017
Ute Wehrle	**Bächle, Gässle, Puppenmord**	2016
Ute Wehrle	**Endstation Schwarzwald**	2019

HISTORISCHE SCHWARZWALD-ROMANE / HISTORICAL NOVELS SET IN THE BLACK FOREST

Ralf H. Dorweiler	**Das Geheimnis des Glasbläsers**	2018
Astrid Fritz	**Die Hexen von Freiburg**	2003
Astrid Fritz	**Die Pestengel von Freiburg**	2011
Astrid Fritz	**Tod im Höllental**	2017
Birgit Hermann	**Die Glasmacherin**	2016
Inge Barth-Grözinger	**Wildblütenzeit. Die große Schwarzwaldsaga**	2018

GEISTESWISSENSCHAFTEN / HUMANITIES

Klaus Theweleit	**Männerphantasien**	1977/78
Martin Heidegger	**Sein und Zeit**	1927
Peter Sloterdijk	**Kritik der zynischen Vernunft**	1983
Edmund Husserl	**Die reine Phänomenologie …**	1916
Erasmus von Rotterdam	**De civilitate morum puerilium**	1530
Heinrich Popitz	**Phänomene der Macht**	1986
Heinrich August Winkler	**Arbeiter und Arbeiterbewegung in der Weimarer Republik**	1984–87
Max Weber	**Der Nationalstaat und die Volkswirtschaftspolitik**	1895
Jens Schäfer	**Gebrauchsanweisung für Freiburg und den Schwarzwald**	2011/2021

Quellen / References

8
Eigene Recherche / *The authors' own research*

10
Eigene Recherche / *The authors' own research*

12
Eigene Recherche / *The authors' own research* • Wikipedia • https://mapcarta.com/

14
Google-Maps • Wikipedia

16
Eigene Recherche / *The authors' own research* • Google-Maps • https://zell-weierbach.de/gemeinde/partnerschaften/usa • Wikipedia • www.bordhunde.com • www.schwarzwaldpalast.de/neuigkeiten-und-angebote/ein-stueck-schwarzwald-in-suedamerika

18
Hubert Klausmann, Konrad Kunze, Renate Schrambke: Kleiner Dialektatlas. Alemannisch und Schwäbisch in Baden-Württemberg. Bühl: Konkordia 1993 • Muettersproch-Gsellschaft, Verein für alemannische Sprache, www.alemannisch.de

20
http://genwiki.genealogy.net • www.namenforschung.net/dfd/woerterbuch/liste/ • Werner König, Renate Schrambke: Die Sprachatlanten des schwäbisch-alemannischen Raumes: Baden-Württemberg, Bayerisch-Schwaben, Elsaß, Liechtenstein, Schweiz, Vorarlberg. Bühl: Konkordia 1999 • Konrad Kunze: dtv-Atlas Namenkunde: Vor- und Familiennamen im deutschen Sprachgebiet. München: dtv 2003

22
www.uhren-park.de • www.schwarzwaldimpressionen.de • www.freudenstadt.de • www.rothaus.de • www.tannenmuehle.de • www.festspielhaus.de • www.franz-schuessele.de • www.schwarzwald-tourismus.info • www.duravit.de • Wikipedia • www.durbach.de • http://film-freiburg-schwarzwald.de/de/location/holzfasskeller-breisach • Winzergenossenschaft Breisach

24
www.nationalpark-schwarzwald.de • https://naturparkschwarzwald.de • www.biosphaerengebiet-schwarzwald.de • www.naturpark-suedschwarzwald.de • www.schwarzwald-tourismus.info

26
Eigene Recherche / *The authors' own research* • Forst Baden-Württemberg, www.forstbw.de • Jens Schäfer: Gebrauchsanweisung für Freiburg und den Schwarzwald. München: Piper 2011 • Landkreis Breisgau-Hochschwarzwald (Hg.): Breisgau-Hochschwarzwald. Verlag Karl Schillinger 1980

28
Eigene Recherche / *The authors' own research* • www.grafenhausen.de (Ortsinfo, Geschichte) • www.schwaebische-post.de/881778/ • Regierungspräsidium Freiburg • www.monumentaltrees.com

30
www.echtle-holz.de/totenbrettchen/ • www.architektur3.de/projekte/kirchturm-bleibach/ • www.holzbau-bruno-kaiser.de • https://floesser-altensteig.de/geschichte-der-floserei-2/

32
www.v-ds.org • www.schwarzwaldpalast.de • www.uhren-park.de • www.hubertherr.de • Wikipedia

34
Fotos: Sebastian Wehrle, www.sebastian-wehrle.de, Kunstgalerie in Freiamt • www.gutach-schwarzwald.de • Wikipedia • www.schwarzwald-kinzigtal.info/kultur/bollenhut • www.vogtsbauernhof.de (Traditionelles Handwerk, Bollenhutmacherin)

36
www.faller.de, Dank an / *Our thanks to* Francisco Hoyo • www.vogtsbauernhof.de • Wikipedia • www.bauforschung-bw.de (Suche / *Search*: Hippenseppenhof)

38
www.hinterwaelder.com • Wikipedia • www.slowfood.de/was-wir-tun/arche-des-geschmacks/die_arche_passagiere/hinterwaelder_rind • www.g-e-h.de • www.asr-rind.de (Rinderrassen, Hinterwälder)

40
www.schwarzwald-tourismus.info • www.asr-rind.de (Rinderrassen, Hinterwälder und Vorderwälder) • www.pferdezucht-rps.de • www.naturpark-suedschwarzwald.de • Wikipedia

42
www.schwarzwaelder-schinken-verband.de • www.schwarzwald-tourismus.info

56
Verwendung der Kartenbilder mit freundlicher Genehmigung der / *Playing card images courtesy of* Spielkartenfabrik Altenburg GmbH, Leipziger Straße 7, D-04600 Altenburg, a Cartamundi Company © 2020 ASS Altenburger Spielkarten • www.cego-online.de • Wikipedia • http://laberlaberlaber.de/cego/

68
Landkreis Breisgau-Hochschwarzwald (Hg.): Breisgau-Hochschwarzwald. Verlag Karl Schillinger 1980 • Regierungspräsidium Freiburg, Landesamt für Geologie, Rohstoffe und Bergbau, https://lgrb-bw.de • Wikipedia • www.karlsruhe.de • www.hagelabwehr-ortenau.de • https://hagelabwehr-suedwest.de

44
Tante / *Aunt* Renate • Eigene Recherche / *The authors' own research*

58
Wikipedia • Jens Schäfer: Gebrauchsanweisung für Freiburg und den Schwarzwald. München: Piper 2011

70
www.schwarzwald.com/karte/bahnlinien.html • Wikipedia • Google Maps • www.bahn.de • https://openrailwaymap.org/ • www.baden-wuerttemberg.de • www.faller.de

46
Websites der Brauereien / *Brewery websites*

60
Wikipedia

72
Websites der einzelnen Ferienstraßen / *Holiday route websites* • www.schwarzwald-tourismus.info

48
www.badischerwein.de • https://naturparkschwarzwald.blog/wie-der-bocksbeutel-nach-baden-kam/ • www.bad-bellingen.de/media/attraktionen/oberrheinisches-baeder-und-heimatmuseum • Wikipedia

62
www.dfb.de • www.scfreiburg.com • www.kicker.de • Wikipedia

74
www.schwarzwaldverein.de, Dank an / *Our thanks to* Mirko Bastian • Wikipedia

50
www.oberkirch.de • www.kleinbrenner-baden.de/brenner • www.myspirits.eu

64
www.scfreiburg.com • www.kicker.de • Kommando Charly Schulz • Wikipedia

76
www.schwarzwald-tourismus.info/entdecken/Wandern/Fernwanderwege • www.schwarzwaldverein.de/wege/fernwanderwege/index.html • Websites einzelner Fernwanderwege / *Websites for the various hiking trails*

52
www.schwarzwald-tourismus.info (Suche / *Search*: Michelin) • www.schwarzwald-tapas.de • Websites der einzelnen Lokale / *Restaurant websites*

66
www.liftverbund-feldberg.de (Erlebnisse, Meilensteine des Skisports) • Wikipedia • www.swr.de (Suche / *Search*: Skier erobern Schwarzwald • www.planet-wissen.de (Suche / *Search*: Georg Thoma)

78
Websites der Türme / *Websites for the various towers* • www.outdooractive.com • www.feldbergbahn.de • www.schwarzwaldportal.com • www.ferienwelt-suedschwarzwald.de • www.landesmuseum.de • Wikipedia • www.duravit.de • Vitra Design Museum • Badisches Landesmuseum Karlsruhe • Kaiserstuhl Touristik e.V. Ihringen

54
Eigene Recherche / *The authors' own research*

80
www.europapark.de, Dank an / Our thanks to Andrea Metzger, Ed Euromaus

90
Websites der einzelnen Kirchen und Klöster / Websites of the various churches and monasteries • Wikipedia • www.hochschwarzwald.de • www.eslam.de

100
Websites der Museen / Museum websites • www.schwarzwald-tourismus.info

82
www.schwaebisch-alemannische-fasnet.de • www.alemannische-seiten.de/schwaebisch-alemannische-fastnacht.php • Larvenfotos: Mit freundlicher Genehmigung der / Mask photos: courtesy of Alemannischen Larvenfreunde – Verein zur Förderung europäischer Maskenkultur e.V., www.larvenfreunde.de/maskenmuseum/, Dank an / Our thanks to Clemens Fuchs, Fotos / Photos: Andreas Reutter (Alemannische Larvenfreunde), Eddy Roßwog

92
www.schwarzwaelder-bote.de (Suche / Search: Longinuskreuz) • Wikipedia • www.alemannische-seiten.de (Suche / Search: Longinuskreuz)

102
Wikipedia • https://franzxaver-winterhalter.wordpress.com/ • www.artnet.de • www.winterhalter-menzenschwand.de • Städtische Museen Freiburg Augustinermuseum (Hg.): Unser Schwarzwald, Romantik und Wirklichkeit. Petersberg: Michael Imhof 2011

94
www.staufen.de (Suche / Search: Hebungsrisse) • Wikipedia • www.staufenstiftung.de • www.deutschlandfunkkultur.de (Suche / Search: Schäden durch Geothermie)

104
www.bbk.bund.de (Aufgaben, Kulturgutschutz, Zentraler Bergungsort) • Wikipedia • www.geschichtsspuren.de

84
Schwarzwald Tourismus GmbH, www.schwarzwald-tourismus.info • Statistisches Landesamt Baden-Württemberg, Stuttgart • Tourismusnetzwerk Baden-Württemberg

96
www.hansgrohe.de • www.junghans.de • www.uhu.de • www.hvg-dgg.de (Museen, Kulturpark Glashütte Buhlbach • Wikipedia • Förderverein Glashütte Buhlbach, www.glashuette-buhlbach-foerderverein.de/was-ist-der-buhlbacher-schlegel • www.technoseum.de

106
Wikipedia • Eigene Recherche / The authors' own research

86
Schwarzwald Tourismus GmbH, www.schwarzwald-tourismus.info

98
www.weltmarktfuehrerindex.de • Websites der einzelnen Firmen / Company websites

108
Eigene Recherche / The authors' own research • Albert-Ludwigs-Universität Freiburg, www.uni-freiburg.de • Dr. Bernhard Lauer, Brüder Grimm-Gesellschaft e.V. • Wolfgang Kaiser

88
Websites der einzelnen Bäder, Städte und Gemeinden / Websites of the various spas, cities and towns • Jens Schäfer: Gebrauchsanweisung für Freiburg und den Schwarzwald. München: Piper 2011